PENGUIN BOOKS

THE SCENE BOOK

Sandra Scofield is the author of seven novels and a memoir. Her novels have received awards including a nomination for the National Book Award, an American Book Award from the Before Columbus Foundation, a National Endowment for the Arts Fellowship, a New American Writing Award, and the Jesse Jones Award for the best fiction from the Texas Institute of Letters. Several of her novels have been named Notable Books of the Year by the *New York Times Book Review.* She is a popular summer workshop instructor for the Iowa Summer Writing Festival and other conferences.

ALSO BY SANDRA SCOFIELD

THE SCENE BOOK

A PRIMER FOR
THE FICTION WRITER

Sandra Scofield

PENGUIN BOOKS

PENGUIN BOOKS

Published by the Penguin Group

Penguin Group (USA) Inc., 375 Hudson Street, New York, New York 10014, U.S.A.
Penguin Group (Canada), 90 Eglinton Avenue East, Suite 700, Toronto, Ontario, Canada M4P 2Y3
(a division of Pearson Penguin Canada Inc.)
Penguin Books Ltd, 80 Strand, London WC2R 0RL, England
Penguin Ireland, 25 St Stephen's Green, Dublin 2, Ireland (a division of Penguin Books Ltd)
Penguin Group (Australia), 250 Camberwell Road, Camberwell, Victoria 3124, Australia
(a division of Pearson Australia Group Pty Ltd)
Penguin Books India Pvt Ltd, 11 Community Centre, Panchsheel Park,
New Delhi–110 017, India
Penguin Books (NZ), cnr Airborne and Rosedale Roads, Albany, Auckland 1310,
New Zealand (a division of Pearson New Zealand Ltd)
Penguin Books (South Africa) (Pty) Ltd, 24 Sturdee Avenue, Rosebank, Johannesburg 2196,
South Africa

Penguin Books Ltd, Registered Offices:
80 Strand, London WC2R 0RL, England

First published in Penguin Books 2007

10   9   8

Copyright © Sandra Scofield, 2007
All rights reserved

Pages 243–47 constitute an extension of this copyright page.

LIBRARY OF CONGRESS CATALOGING-IN-PUBLICATION DATA
Scofield, Sandra Jean, 1943–
The scene book : a primer for the fiction writer / Sandra Scofield.
p.   cm.
Includes bibliographical references.
ISBN 978-0-14-303826-9
1. Fiction—authorship. 2. Narration (Rhetoric) I. Title.
PN3383.N35S36 2007
808.3—dc22 2006044848

Printed in the United States of America
Set in Bembo
Designed by Elke Sigal

CONTENTS

INTRODUCTION:
THE READING WRITER

The principles that guided the development of this
book. (In some ways, the introduction is about you.)

- A few words about the author
- The idea of the book
- Thoughts on talent and apprenticeship

About me

I learned about writing the hard way, without classes or a mentor, yet writing never felt hard. From the time I was a little girl until after my own child was a toddler, I wrote because it was a natural thing to do, something that gave me pleasure—the way that gardening or playing the piano does for other people—with no thought of publishing. The impulse to put stories on the page was so strong I would feel it physically, the way you have to get out of the house to take a walk. I wish I still had the stamina I had then, when I could work all night, hardly eating or sleeping. What I wanted, I see now, was to enter another world—the life of the scene. I wanted to watch characters work out their destinies on the page. I would grow very excited waiting for a story to reach its final image; I never knew what it would be before I got there. Writing was in some way another form of reading and an extension of my dreams.

I grew up with no television and I saw very few movies until I was a young adult. My instincts for shaping stories came from my experience of reading books in my childhood, like the Nancy

Drew mysteries, the adventure stories of Richard Halliburton and Jack London, and novels like *The Silver Chalice, Cheaper by the Dozen,* and *Ramona.* By seventh grade I was reading a lot of short stories and narrative poems. At fifteen, when my mother was dying, I escaped into the war novels of Erich Maria Remarque and the novels of Thomas Hardy. I went on to read piles of old-fashioned fiction, with its fine diction and leisurely pace. I loved Trollope, Arnold Bennett, E. M. Forster, and other writers to whom I was introduced in my formal education. There were living writers, too, whose work moved me as a young adult reader and drove me forward out of the nineteenth century: men, at first, like Philip Roth (*Goodbye, Columbus; Letting Go*), Paul Bowles (*The Sheltering Sky*), Albert Camus (especially his journals). I fell in love with Eudora Welty's characters, while I admired Mary McCarthy for her arch intellect and wit. I can remember exactly where I was sitting on the day I began reading Joyce Carol Oates's *them.*

Later, in the back pages of the magazine *Redbook,* I encountered writers like Marge Piercy, Toni Morrison, and Margaret Atwood. I discovered the annual fiction anthologies. By then I was a young working mother, doing most of my writing in my head or in short bursts after I got the baby to sleep.

I tell you these things so that you can see how innocently I made my way, not understanding for a very long time that the doors into writing were not closed. (Published writers were, to me, mythical creatures.) At some point I began to want my work to be better than what I could create in one-time sessions on my portable typewriter. I knew that I needed to learn skills and that I had to have criteria for evaluating my work: Did I rush? Was I too obvious? Did I open in the right place?

I began to read in a new way. I dog-eared pages and underlined passages. I copied paragraphs into a notebook. I studied stories as if they were puzzles I had been given to solve. I developed a vocabulary of plain words to describe what I discerned from the way other authors structured their narratives.

At first my discoveries were basic, even naïve. It dawned on me one day that I could do without all the fancy work around the word *said*. I began to notice the various strategies used to indicate transitions of time.

I came to believe that what readers care about most are characters, and that what they remember best are images and action.

Slowly, over years, I developed what I think of as craft, the practiced, deliberate way of choosing how to say things in order to reach the desired effect. I'd like to share some of what I've learned with you.

About the book—and you

I do have a sense of a "you" out there: a reader curled on the couch late at night, or sitting at a table in the early morning before work; another walking briskly around the neighborhood, thinking about a story. Some of you take classes or go to workshops, and some have the support of a critique group, but I suspect that many of you are as I was: solitary, a little foggy, but hopeful and determined. (I should say, as I am.)

You have stories you want to tell, things you want to say, characters who whisper in your ear, but you have problems, too, and you would like some help. You already know the old saw about writing being more perspiration than inspiration, and you know about drafting and revising. You've made sacrifices to block out serious time for your work. What you need now is something specific and practical, something to help you think like a writer. You are willing to slave away, if someone will just part the curtains a little.

That's what I hope to offer you.

Many aspects of writing fiction can't be described well, let alone directly taught, but scenes have identifiable elements that can be analyzed. I can't tell you how to write your stories, of course. Some writers would say nobody can tell you anything at all, but they tend to be really good writers who don't understand mere mortals like us. So I'll just tell you some of the things I have learned about scenes, and you can move on from there.

I don't claim that the observations I make represent the thinking of the writers whose work I use as examples; maybe they wrote with intuitive genius or with a process I can't fathom. Yet I think you can study others' writing, identify useful elements of craft, and apply them in your own work, and I'm not alone in this belief. The Canadian story writer Alice Munro says that she enters others' stories wherever she has a notion, as one enters a room in a house. She connects this habit to her ideas about building up a story of her own around its "soul" in a way that leads to its structure.

Many esteemed writers have paid homage to their own chosen models: Raymond Carver to Chekhov and Hemingway; F. Scott Fitzgerald to Conrad and Joyce; Flannery O'Connor to Sophocles and Nathanael West.

You will find that this book does not push you toward any particular style, something I think would be impossible. Writers use scenes in their own way, just as they use language in their own way. Some build stories with scenes like Legos piled one on the other. Others weave them in slippery ways.

The models are various and fine and your choices are many. I know that there is a tendency to *read about* strategies and think that now they're in your quiver. I have to say this: Plowing through exercises, choosing your own models, keeping a notebook, trying to incorporate new skills—these are the ways you learn. I urge you to work without rushing.

Be patient. All arts—painting, playing a violin, blowing glass—are built on solid practice. Doing the exercises really does bake the batter.

By the way, I don't want you to think that I am telling you that every story is made of a rosary of scenes. Once, popular fiction was mostly composed this way, and much genre fiction still is, but it's a pretty old-fashioned strategy. Nevertheless, if you know how to construct dramatic, interesting, effective scenes, you'll understand a lot about how to make stories work. Maybe some of your early work will be a bit cobbled together or overwritten, but whose work starts out perfectly? In time, understanding the way that the *sense of the scene* underlies narrative will put you in control of your story. You can wind your way in and out of fragments of scenes, stop to summarize and comment, drop in bits of dialogue, muse and question and jump around in time, while your work will resound with the underlying images, actions, and meanings of inherent scenes. There will always be that ghost of the structure to hold the story together. Some writers come to this naturally, and so some writers and teachers think there's no point in teaching about scenes, that it's a natural skill. I say: lucky writers, pessimistic teachers.

I've never had a student tell me it was a waste of time to work on scenes. And in a workshop or class, I've never had two students come up with the same product when they did the same exercise. In fact, I encourage you to bring in a bit of subterfuge to the exercises—your quixotic, cheeky, unique way of seeing things. I offer my guidelines in the spirit of that new invention, the bicycle with training wheels that pull in to make a two-wheeler when the pedaler gets up to speed.

I will:

1. Help you recognize how much you already know about scenes.
2. Explain important basic principles about the way scenes work.
3. Introduce you to concepts you can use in planning or evaluating your own scenes.
4. Show you models that demonstrate those concepts in a wide variety of styles.
5. Suggest numerous exercises to help you develop a repertoire of skills.
6. Give you guides to studying scenes as models.
7. Suggest further reading you can do to study how esteemed authors have used scenes in exemplary ways.

So you will know:

- How scenes work.
- How you can study authors' scenes.
- How you can make *your* scenes work.

You can use this book studying alone. If you belong to a group, you can do exercises together and bring in models to share. You can use the concepts to talk about one another's drafts. (There are evaluation guides on pp. 186 to 188.)

I have drawn from a variety of contemporary writers with a range of styles. Except for E. M. Forster, I have not turned to the so-called classic writers (e.g., Chekhov, Austen, Conrad) because such writers are already widely and well discussed. I hope that my examples will encourage you to find your own. I have explained each example so that it is not necessary for you to have the complete story to understand the concept, though you may occasionally want to look up the original text. I provide two very different stories for study, with some questions to prompt you, and in the section "Further Reading," pp. 229 to 235, I talk about stories or novels that are easily found in libraries and bookstores, so that you can go to those sources if you want more extended examples.

Little by little, you should acquire a collection of books that serve you as a reading writer—books that you can mark up and come back to. If you can't afford to buy them all new (and some will be out of print), there are many sources of used or remaindered books, including local used bookstores and online stores.*

Balance your writing practice with focused reading of writers whose work you admire, and work to expand your reading. Over time, you will form your own sound judgment about what is good, and set your goals according to what you like and what you want to write. Don't get trapped in a false choice between "literary" and "commercial" writing. In my mind, fiction exists on a continuum of accessibility, affected primarily by language (style) and story complexity. Different readers prefer work on

---

* Notice that I say to buy used when you can't buy new, and *not* galleys that are being sold in used bookstores, often when a book is just out. Please don't support this practice, which profits neither author nor publisher. It isn't what you would want done with your book.

different parts of the continuum, but surely no writer wants to be inaccessible, nor does another want to be simplistic. Most of us strive to write the best we can for the widest audience we can reach. Some of us happen to love plot and action more than layers of meaning or intricacies of language; some would rather spend more time on each page, musing as the story slowly moves along.

I think that a lot of so-called literary fiction founders when its authors fail to consider the readers' need to grasp the story line. I also believe that mainstream fiction is best when it develops complexities, whether every reader "gets" them or not. It's not that unusual to see the best of both approaches wed in popular books. Think of novels by Jane Hamilton, Dennis Lehane, Anne Tyler, Diane Johnson, Karen Joy Fowler, Margaret Atwood, Ron Hansen, and a host of other commercially successful, critically admired writers. I'm sure you can make a long list of successful authors whose work you admire for its artistry. You may also find that the authors you admire most are underappreciated. Should you then learn from them? By all means! If they seem to be good models to you, they are. I take pride in discovering and supporting writers who aren't (yet?) famous, and I trust my own taste. (And when I say "support" I mean I buy books, lots of books.)

Back to models. What of those amazing writers whose techniques dazzle you? The ones you can't believe came up with *that*. In time you will find you can analyze their writing, too, but, practically, what's the point? You wouldn't want to be identified as copying them, even if you could. Read them for pleasure; you'll pick up things you aren't aware of absorbing.

With practice, you will find yourself identifying scenes and their functions—and their beauty—easily, even automatically, a habit that will pay off in your own writing.

The exercises in this book are not intended to replace the intuitive process that moves you into and through the early drafts of a story, but when you are ready to look coolly at what you have produced, you should find that you are able to fit words around the way you have constructed and embellished scenes, and that you can identify problems you want to solve in revision. The emphasis here is on writing major scenes—the ones that carry the story—although fragments ("pieces") of scenes are often embedded in narrative or used elliptically, and minor scenes augment the main story line. Not every scene can or should have the same weight.*

Many contemporary short story writers write whole stories without ever using a fully developed scene, but I don't think that's a good place for you to start unless that's your natural inclination and talent, and if it is, you probably aren't going to be doing the exercises in this book anyway. What you may find is that if you construct a solid sequence of scenes in one of your early drafts (like a painter doing studies), you will then be comfortable with a freer narrative flow that darts in and out of the scenes, letting them assume a more subtle role in the narrative play. It's something like building a house with lots of long sight lines, rooms with fewer walls and doors. The more you read with this in mind, the more you will understand what I mean by "embedded scenes" and "elliptical scenes" and "scene fragments."

If you find yourself, in narrative summaries or within scenes, referring to events that happened before the time of the story, it will probably help you to stop and write the important prior scenes, even though you may not "use them." This gives you a firm grasp of your story history. Such prior scenes may never find their way into the text of your story, but knowing them will keep you from stopping your story dead in its tracks to make up the past as you go along. (How many lines of thought can you handle at one time anyway?)

In short, when you're exploring your story, don't be shy about doing so in scenes that help you understand where your story

---

* When you use a scene fragment, the whole is suggested by the part. So be sure you know what that whole is and why you have chosen the segment.

came from. It's not a waste of time to write things that don't end up in the final version.

Inspiration, analysis, reflection, restructuring, rewriting, and editing are different parts of a grand process we call writing. Demystifying that process will give you a greater sense of control over your work. Be patient, optimistic, and determined. Good luck!

About talent and apprenticeship

Many people question the whole enterprise of teaching writing, and it is indeed an enterprise these days, with hundreds of college programs, writing conferences, online courses, and numerous books. Elements of craft can be demonstrated, as they are in every art form, but talent is another matter.

We could convene a symposium just to try to define talent. I think of it this way: A person with a talent for writing has a sound grasp of language, a love of words, and a natural "narrative faculty," a term I borrow from William Sloane in his wonderful little classic, *The Craft of Writing.* That faculty comprises a love of storytelling and a gift for recognizing, remembering, inventing, and telling stories—a gift you surely have if you are driven to write. It is an aspect of talent you can cultivate by immersing yourself in more reading, and in reading more diverse stories, such as those by ethnic and immigrant writers, foreign writers, and other tellers of stories far from your experience.

Technique, on the other hand, can be taught, practiced, and learned, whether it is constructing a scene or learning to use repetition for emphasis. My experience has been that an odd thing happens in craft workshops: As writers practice skills, their "talent" flowers.

So what should you do?

Start by doing an honest assessment of your writing.* Show

---

* Sometimes the best strategy is to pay someone to do this if you think you will make a friend uncomfortable or you will hold criticism against him. Only you know how tender your feelings are.

someone you trust a piece of your work that you have taken as far as you can. Don't ask for a critique of the story at this point. Ask, instead: Can you follow my logic? Am I making mistakes in grammar, diction, or spelling? Do I ramble and get off focus? Does my vocabulary seem up to the job? Where is there grace, precision, beauty in my sentences, and where are there clunkers? Would you identify some good sentences or passages? Some weak ones? What do you think I do best?

If you are weak, work to get strong. And get a tough skin! You aren't going to learn from false compliments—and you sure won't get any from agents, editors, or readers. On a couple of occasions I have worked with students in creative writing who had problems of usage and who were offended when I pointed them out. They felt that dangling participles and lack of agreement between nouns and verbs were minor concerns to be dealt with in editing. I disagree.

Frank Conroy, a masterful writer and famed teacher who was long the director of the Writers' Workshop at the University of Iowa, used to begin his examination of student texts in workshops at what he called the "microlevel of language," the words and sentences. Clarity and precision at that level are the bedrock of narrative. If you don't think your sentences are up to the work, get some help from a retired English teacher or a recommended grad student or a good composition textbook. And consider hiring a professional copy editor for your manuscripts before you submit them.

Millions of immigrants have come to this country and mastered the English language; some of them have become outstanding writers. Pulitzer Prize–winning poet Lisel Mueller arrived as a teenager, speaking German. Ha Jin, who won the National Book Award, came here in his twenties, after serving in the Chinese military. Lara Vapnyar emigrated from Russia to New York in 1994 and began publishing short stories in English in 2002. They are amazing people, and they certainly demonstrate the kind of grit writers need.

Oregon author Katherine Dunn tells the story of how she decided, years ago, that she wasn't good enough to go on writing—

even though she had already published several novels. So she spent years practicing from writing textbooks until she felt she had it right. Then she wrote *Geeks,* a National Book Award finalist.

A friend of mine asked for my advice about learning to write novels. I suggested she study a book I like, *A Farm Under a Lake,* by Martha Bergland; their sensibilities seemed similar. My friend structured her story using Bergland's chapters one by one to lay out scenes. In the end, her novel was very much her own, she had a story she was proud of, and she had learned a lot. Now she is working on a new novel.

Victor Villaseñor, author of *Rain of Gold,* the popular book about his parents' immigration from Mexico, told me that he can't write a literate first draft. Every page requires a struggle with his dyslexia, so he just keeps at it; story first, then language, all by hand on yellow pages for a long time.

I've heard numerous published writers say they write ten, twelve, fifteen drafts of stories before they even know what they're about. Raymond Carver was famous for his self-described doggedness.

Who is talented? Aren't all of these writers? Talent seems to consist in great part of desire and persistence. (Stephen King struck out four times before *Carrie*.) I love to hear about writers who write for personal satisfaction and are surprised when they discover how good their stories are. That's one of the reasons I enjoy summer workshops, where people arrive brimming with stories and a passion for hearing and telling them.

We are not beginners forever, but we never stop learning. Unlike the medieval shoemaker or the contemporary jeweler, the writer does not report to a studio and a master, does not put in time and graduate to a license. The apprenticeship is self-directed.

I think of myself as having a kind of conversation with writers whom I admire as I read their work. I read reviews and criticism, too, and I keep up with the ideas of those who are teaching. (Subscriptions to *The Writer's Chronicle,* from the Associated Writing Programs, and to *Poets & Writers* are a fine place to start.) I am constantly trying out techniques and testing concepts against my own work. Often there is a tug-of-war between my admiration for writers and my disagreement with their assertions. I think this benefits me because it makes me form and question tenets of my own.

The terms of one's learning shift as one progresses. We improve incrementally. This is my advice:

1. Think of yourself as a worker.
2. Show up at the job.

The writing teacher Janet Burroway, author of *Writing Fiction: A Guide to Narrative Craft*, a widely used writing text, says, "Good writing comes from an ability to connect the interior richness of which all of us are possessed—*all*—with the structure of the language."

Some are lucky and acquire that facility at a very young age, with little effort. They are prodigies. The rest of us run to catch up. One way or the other, you get somewhere you haven't been before.

PART ONE

THE SCENE PRIMER
SENSE AND STRUCTURE

1

THE BASICS

BASIC CONCEPTS ABOUT SCENES

RECOGNIZE HOW MUCH YOU ALREADY KNOW ABOUT
SCENES AND IDENTIFY SOME BASIC CONCEPTS ABOUT THEM.

- WHY ARE SCENES SO POWERFUL?
- WHAT IS A SCENE?
- WHAT ARE FOUR BASIC SCENE ELEMENTS?
- EXERCISES

Why are scenes so powerful?

The scene is the most vivid and immediate part of story,
the place where the reader is the most emotionally involved,
the part that leaves the reader with images and a memory
of the action.

Many occasions and events stand out in our minds and we swear we can remember just what happened, moment by moment. How many times have you heard someone say, "I walked in on such a scene!" Such occasions are memorable because people interacted in emotional, eventful ways.

You probably talk about other kinds of scenes that you observed— like the mother-child quarrel in a grocery store aisle that made you uneasy because it went on a little too long. Or the magical moment on your beach vacation when you heard tinkling sounds and children singing and then suddenly the children passed by you, all of them with masks and homemade instruments—bells, combs, and rattles. You remember that the sun was just setting. In fact, you don't really know what happened. You just know that you were there for it.

When you observe something happening but you are not involved, even if you see only a part of the incident, you sense the thrall of story; you are passing or intersecting a scene that someone else is playing out. We do this often. Writers notice such moments.

Recently as I waited at an intersection behind several cars, I noticed on my right a driveway in which a woman was standing by a car. The hatchback was open, and her arms were crossed in front of her. She looked so stricken, I felt a pang. Just as I pulled away, I saw a man come to the car and throw a box in the back. I thought of that scene all day. What had happened between the man and the woman? Was he leaving, and would he come back? Was there some bitter necessity separating them or was anger fueling his action?

Our memories are filled with images that are doors into old scenes in our lives. A few years ago I happened to be working on an early draft of a memoir about my teen years, when I turned on the television late one night and caught an old movie with Sandra Dee. Just the sight of her round pretty face brought back the memory of the night at the movies when I quarreled with my first boyfriend—because he accused me of being jealous of her. When I got back to my writing, a wealth of details poured onto the page. That recalled incident became an important part of explaining who I was at fifteen, and because I saw the Sandra Dee movie so many years later, I was able to reconstruct a scene in a car at a drive-in theater.

Tap into your own sense of scene. Make it a habit to extend those moments that catch your eye; follow fragmentary memories back to the place where they hold story. If you are in a writing group, consider an occasional warm-up exercise of telling scenes, no more than three or four minutes each. Think: beginning, middle, end. Don't digress too much.

Other scenes that stay with us are those from movies we have loved, because they are full of heightened emotion and they are visually powerful. List scenes that you have liked, and then try to analyze what was so appealing. You will see that, above all else, *something happened;* films are built of linked scenes that move a story forward toward its consequences and resolution. Usually, we remember the high moment, or culmination of a sequence of events, i.e., a sequence of scenes. Sometimes it is a tense moment of action, such as when an athlete wins against all odds, or lovers part because great events around them make their union impossible. Memorable scenes aren't always made of big action, of course. Often they are those times when the story slows down and we experience the characters in intimate moments. Notice how much we can feel without being told exactly what the characters are feeling.

All too often, the apprentice fiction writer gets caught up in the thoughts of characters and forgets to make something happen in a scene. The writer forgets that *actions cause reactions.* Narrative is sensory and active, and movies exploit those aspects of story.

Written narrative is rich in a different way, because the writer can delve into more aspects of an experience than a movie can, taking us deep into the souls of characters—balanced with and illuminating action. We are able to share in the memories and digressive consciousness of characters (think of Virginia Woolf and Chekhov). Because images are seen only in the mind, readers have to participate in the process of the story. And the writer has immense latitude in moving about in time and space, confident that the reader will follow.

So, although there are things to be learned from screenwriting about developing characters and stories, I don't recommend trying to learn narrative structure from screenplays. Hollywood loves a formula, and that's not what you need. (Most good indie films ignore the formula.) And you don't want to turn to movie memories for images to use in your fiction, any more than you would use passages from other writers' books.

There are ways to use movies to your advantage as an apprentice writer. I've already mentioned looking at the ways character is revealed through action. And as a moviegoer, you know that viewers expect a certain amount of speed and spectacle, so, without undercutting your own sensibility, you can keep the likely impatience of readers in mind. If you recognize that you have a tendency to wander, keep an eye on the distance between moments of action. One way is to intersperse long passages of narration with vivid bits from scenes. Short story writers have to be deft at this because it is economical, something the form demands.

Movies are also good source material for writing practice. If there are particular movie scenes that you love, watch them over and over and try writing them as if they are scenes in a novel. This frees you from having to make things up, so that you can concentrate on how to convey what happened. What went by so quickly on the screen will take you much longer to put on the page, because the visual aspects have to be conveyed in words. You will have to integrate all that description with the action— a great exercise—and you will, almost involuntarily, emphasize event over emotion, that is, the external over the internal. Again, a good exercise. At the same time, you can do what the screenwriter couldn't do, which is to employ character interiority* as one aspect of emotional response. You can turn the movie scene into prose fiction. (Do not turn to the "novelized movie" books for models. They're just scripts written out a bit.)

If you enjoy doing this, some screenplays are published, and you can use the dialogue and develop the rest. It doesn't really matter if you have the dialogue right, though, as long as you write a scene you are pleased with.

Here are some screenplays that I suggest because they have scenes that transfer to thinking in prose.

---

* Interiority is the reflection and musing that the character does without speaking his or her thoughts; this may include thinking about not only the present action but also triggered memories and flashback scenes.

Recommended Movies

BABETTE'S FEAST

Based on a story by Isak Dinesen (Karen Blixen), this would be an interesting film to look at after you work through chapter 11, "Big Scenes." It involves the preparation of a lavish feast by a French refugee who has won the lottery and spends it all to thank the Danes who took her in. Trying to convey the puzzlement of the repressed Danes will challenge you! Capture the horror of the "devout sisters," surveying the kitchen, who consider the rich food a sign of witchery and who vow to eat but not to taste the rich fare. Since it's not in English, you can focus on the sensuality of the scenes.

THE BREAKFAST CLUB

Five high school students meet in Saturday detention. Pick the scene that you enjoyed the most and try to convey the action crisply. I'd pick one of the main characters and focus on him or her enough that you feel you can write a scene and make up the dialogue (you know the essence of the scene from watching it) without trying to copy exactly what was in the film. In this way, you practice observing and then translating into prose. It doesn't matter if it's faithful to the script.

THE CRYING GAME

This movie was famous for outing the "girlfriend" as transgendered, but that's not the part I recommend. If you're interested in writing action scenes, study the opening scenes of this movie, when the IRA captures a black British soldier. Plan the scene sequence, spelling out the beats of action, i.e., each step in the rush of the kidnapping. Then write one of the scenes. You might want to try your hand at rendering the poor guy's terror once he's in enemy hands.

DESERT BLOOM

A classic coming-of-age film in which a girl learns about herself and her troubled father, a veteran, during the time of the Nevada bomb testing in the fifties. Scenes range from intimate, poignant ones between the girl and her visiting aunt to the father's violent outbursts at his family. Jon Voigt and Ellen Barkin are especially good, with great emotional gestures for you to convey with words. The movie is structured in a patchwork of scenes, and there are many that are developed well enough for study. Try a quieter one, such as between the aunt and the girl, and then one with Voigt in high gear. There's one where he tears up his study, and then one where he blows up at his family.

DIRT

(This is the Nancy Savoca movie about the lives of those who clean up after rich people in New York, not the comedy by the same name.) The main character is a Salvadorean woman. The movie is a visual feast and perfect for our purposes, because it is focused on character rather than spectacle. Every scene would serve you; at the very least, pick two or three that contrast in setting, number of people in the scene, emotional tone, etc. There's a wonderful little scene in a kitchen when the maid looks for a sponge and finds a whole drawer full of them. She starts to take a couple for herself, and then has an attack of conscience. There are some sexy scenes with her husband. There are scenes in El Salvador as well as on the Upper East Side of New York.

HUD

There's a barroom fight and a pig-wrestling contest; good luck! Wonderful sexual banter. Big scenes outdoors with sick Mexican cattle. And a young, gorgeous Paul Newman. The opening is a great scene sequence, with a teenage boy looking for Newman after a night of carousing.

STAND BY ME

Try to capture in words the early scene with the boys walking down the rails. You've got a wonderful range of kid "types" and great conflict between the good kids and the bullies as they all try to find the body of someone who was killed by a train. You can have fun hinting at the fifties setting, too. No fair looking at the original Stephen King text!

TENDER MERCIES
There is a beautiful old-fashioned dunking baptism scene in this film, about halfway through. Nice subtle early scenes that show the tentative respect growing between two lonely people. Many good possibilities because the film is about character growth.

YOU CAN COUNT ON ME
A wonderful little movie about a single mother and her messed-up brother. There are so many terrific scenes: between the brother and his sister's precocious son; between the woman and her boss (the fling); a marriage proposal from her boyfriend. Lots of novelists try to write about "ordinary people," and they don't seem to understand that you have to write nuance and incremental change. This screenwriter did. Pick a scene and watch for both elements, then try to put them into words.

WITNESS
A beautifully crafted screenplay, this unusual Hollywood film also offers a wide variety of kinds of scenes, from one-on-ones to expanses of wheat fields. My favorite scene to write would be when the little boy is taken to the police station, wanders around, and recognizes the bad guy in a photo on the wall. Challenge yourself and write the scene in which the folks build a barn in a day.

Memorable Prose Scenes
Of course what you really want is to write terrific prose scenes, so you will want to find examples that have impressed you. Recently I made a trip with my husband from Oregon to Montana and along the way I posed the question to him: What scenes from your reading come to mind as memorable? We went back and forth, de-

lighted not only by the pleasure of our recollections but also by the discovery that we had each read just about everything mentioned by the other. (I guess you could call ours a reading marriage.)

I will mention just a few of these passages, but I am not going to insert scenes. I would rather send you to the original works to read them in context. I hope my list will inspire you to make your own.

ALL THE PRETTY HORSES

We passed a hundred miles retelling favorite scenes from the Cormac McCarthy Border Trilogy. Among lots of dark scenes was one comic one, early on. Two Texas teenagers riding into Mexico meet up with a geeky younger kid, Blevins. They wish they hadn't, but they feel some responsibility for him. A huge thunderstorm is coming and they tell him to take cover, the best they all can. He ignores their advice and rides on; he's so terrified of lightning, he wants to try to outrun it. There's such a great scene sequence. First they find him crouched under some tree roots with all his clothes off—he's afraid his snaps will draw lightning—and he won't come out even when the boys tell him he could drown in such a low place. When they next come upon him he's walking along in a washed-out gulley and he's lost one of his boots, a darned hard thing for a cowboy. He's naked except for his shorts. And worst of all, he's lost his horse.

We also love the opening scene sequence of the second book in the trilogy, *The Crossing*. It concerns the hunt for a Mexican wolf that has crossed the border, and it has a mesmerizing mythic quality in its evocation of the landscape and of the relationship between the young tracker and the wily, beautiful wolf.

CAT'S EYE

Margaret Atwood writes about an artist, Elaine, returning to her hometown for an exhibition after many years away. Her memories of childhood cruelty at the hands of a clique of girls led by Cordelia come back. In a ravine, where she has been warned not to go—"There might be men there"—Cordelia goes beyond bullying to a kind of cold torment that marks Elaine forever—and also gives her motifs for her art. The image of Elaine lying, icy cold, by the side of the creek, unable to help herself until she sees a vision of the Virgin Mary—well, it's a memorable scene!

Our daughter had a hard time with a little clique in third grade, so this story really drove home. (They weren't Atwood bad, though!)

A FLAG FOR SUNRISE
Robert Stone's novel is Graham Greene territory—a fictional Latin American country run by right-wing military despots. It's a novel of extremities, so there are lots of good scenes. A great one is when Frank, the CIA-hired anthropologist spy, is on a diving expedition off a coral reef. At 120 feet he senses something "primordial." A shark, of course, "a silence within a silence." It's scary in its own right, and it has all kinds of double meanings in relation to other characters.

RABBIT, RUN
Generally I don't recommend John Updike to apprentice writers because he's erudite and long-winded, but this book is a jewel and it's full of fabulous scenes. This one is heartbreaking: Harry Angstrom's wife, Janice, has had a very bad day, not much helped by drinking. She has one baby down, her mother is coming over, the apartment is a mess, and the other baby, Rebecca, is dirty. So she puts her in the bathtub. "The water wraps around her forearms like two large hands; under her eyes the pink baby sinks down like a gray stone." The scene is written in a gush, like a terrible dream you can't escape. It is unforgettable.

THE LAST TEMPTATION OF CHRIST
This novel, by Nikos Kazantzakis, is another book that is crammed with powerful scenes, one right after the other. I was raised on stories of a gentle Jesus, and I read this book in my late

teens, so it was a shock to me to discover the furious prophet of
the novel. This scene comes after he has raised Lazarus from the
dead and everyone is having a fit about it, including Jesus himself: "The moment had come. This was the sign he had been
waiting for. The hopelessly rotted world was a Lazarus." Jesus then
jumps up on a platform, uttering a savage cry, surrounded by the
rabble. He tells the crowd that he has come with a sword. He says
that those who follow him have to abandon everything. He de-
clares a new world order. It's big stuff. It's a scene about what he
has to say—but for me, it was vivid. I felt I was in that place, and
I was transfixed, a very impressionable young adult immensely
moved by the passion of this Greek writer.

What is a scene?

Scene is ACTION.

Narrative is the telling of a story (events with consequences
for characters).

> Scenes are those passages in narrative when we slow down
> and focus on an event in the story so that we are "in the
> moment" with characters in action.

Or we can say that a scene is a segment of story told in detail, the
opposite of summarizing. (For purposes of practice, it is useful to
remember that you can read a scene or think of a scene and compress or summarize it as a way to think and talk about it easily.
You would elaborate it in order to turn the summary back into
scene.)

Long or short, covering time compressed or stretched, scene is
event: something happening. It is not description or information
or rumination alone, although any of those things may be a part
of it. And though the scene moves in on action, it is shaped into
an artful representation of life rather than being true to life. That's

why dialogue, for example, is sharper, shorter, smarter than real talk, with all its "uh's" and "well's" and "so's." Dialogue must accomplish something, must move the story. Dialogue has to be part of what is happening.

I find it helpful to think of scenes as little stories. Some are funny and some are sad. Some move fast and some move leisurely. Some are short and some are long. (Often a story has a short passage that "sets a scene," or introduces some information in a close-in way, without going into real action. Such a passage is *scenic* more than it is a *scene*. I'll discuss this in chapter 8, "Images.") Essentially, something must have shifted in your understanding or feelings about a story if a scene has done its work.

Screenwriters live and breathe by scenes, of course, so in their craft books you find much discussion of them. The screenwriter Christopher Keane defines the scene as "an event in a screenplay that occupies time and space." Any change of setting or time marks a new scene. A screenwriter interprets this differently from a prose writer, but the concept is quite useful because it reminds you to let the reader know that there is time and space. I have often read passages in manuscripts that do not let the reader know where the characters are or what time of day it is.

Keane emphasizes, as do playwrights, that a scene has to have a beginning, middle, and end, and that it must be sharply focused. He says that a scene sequence is connected by a "single idea." That is a useful concept, that there is a single driving force through the scenes in a sequence, and that there is an idea or force connecting the sequences into the larger idea of the film or story or novel or play.

In a film, words are the least important element in a scene. In a play, words are probably the most important. In prose, you have the perfect opportunity to meld action and thought and images, all with words. You have more flexibility than a writer in any other genre, being able to come in close, cut across time, combine summary and scene, stop to reflect, and so on. You call up in the reader's mind what playwrights and filmmakers put in front of the viewer.

This is what is common to all stories in all genres and media: *Each part of the story is there for a purpose that serves the story as a whole.*

I'm convinced that having this idea in the front of your mind at all times will do more to keep you on track than anything else I can tell you. It provides a criterion for inclusion and exclusion, for amplification or compression:

How does this scene matter to the story?

Four basic scene elements . . .

1. Every scene has *event* and *emotion*.
2. Every scene has a *function*.
3. Every scene has a *structure*.
4. Every scene has a *pulse*.

. . . restated as guiding principles

1. In a scene, there is *event* and *emotion*.

Or we could say: *In a scene, characters do things and feel things.*
Or we could say: *In a scene, characters act and react.*

So, putting these different ways of saying the same thing together, we can say: *In a scene, characters do things (act and react) that "add up" meaningfully; and they feel things (have emotional and intellectual responses to the action). Thus, every scene has* event *and* emotion.

When you look at your well-written scene, you can state in summary what the events and emotions are; though reductive, this is a kind of acid test of whether the scene has clarity and focus. Even if the scene is "broken up" throughout a longer passage of narrative, you can state the event and emotion developed in it.

Think of action and feeling as Mutt and Jeff, hot and cold, sun and moon. The two go hand in hand. It is possible to write a scene that is all action, without stating what is going on in anyone's mind, but, even then, you will be able to draw conclusions about how the characters have responded by what they do. It is not possible to write a key scene with no action, though the number of words devoted to the action may be less than the words given to description or to character reflection.

Without action, you can have reflection; you can have what amounts to a kind of essayist's voice commenting on the story; you can have a scenic setup; but you don't have a scene. You have a passage of narrative or authorial commentary—one that works in a different way, we hope, and not a failed scene. Please understand that such passages are often some of the most powerful parts of a narrative, but they do not carry the action of the story (unless they brilliantly compress scenes as part of their narrative strategy). They carry emotion and insight, and they give perspective on character, time, and the scope of the story. They add density. Events may be mentioned in summary, even "tossed away" in the telling of a grand tale, but it is in scene that you capture the hearts and imaginations of your readers.

2. Every scene has a *function* in the narrative.

There is a reason the passage is rendered in detail rather than summarized. There is a reason why it appears where it does in the sequence of events. It accomplishes something for the story. It changes something. It makes *now* different from *the past.*

Does your scene serve a function?

- Does it introduce new plot elements?
- Does it reveal something about a character, perhaps making the reader feel more deeply attached to the protagonist?
- Does it set up a situation that will be important in a later scene?
- Do you really need the scene, rather than a summary?

3. Every scene has a *structure:* a beginning, middle, and end.

An alternative way to think of the scene structure is this: There is a situation at the beginning, a line of action, *and then there is a new situation at the end.* Thus, the scene establishes each of these three parts.

One component may be no more than a line or two, the rest implied, but it is there. The scene brings us in, lets us know what is going on, involves us, and lets us go (even if abruptly so).

Forget for the moment that there is such a thing as a scene fragment or that a fragment might be embedded in a narrative summary. In both cases, you have plucked part of the scene from a phantom whole, like a stanza from a song, or a cropped photograph. It is all you need in those circumstances, but as a writer, you know the scene from which you have chosen a part, and the ghost of it hovers over the passage, imparting hints of meaning to the reader. Sometimes it is the richness of what isn't told that makes what is so effective.

In a key scene, a full scene, we have a mini-story. We can see that it starts and stops. A sentence or phrase alerts us. A paragraph orients us, or perhaps begins the action right away. Whatever the strategy, we know the scene has started. We can take a broad-tipped pen and draw a box around it.

Scenes can begin and end in many ways: abruptly, languidly, elaborately, succinctly, obliquely, plainly. You would do well to start a collection of models of beginning sentences and paragraphs. Watch how they work, how they orient you, set you up for what is coming. For now it is enough to remember that scenes are crafted from the very first sentence. They begin, rather than ooze.

I am not being metaphorical about the boxes. When you draw them around your scenes, you will know better what it is you are evaluating. *You can put your finger on your scene(s).* You will know if you have the balance you want between summary and scene, and among types of scenes. You will have identified portions of your story that become objects and that will take away much of the mystery and frustration of revision. You can work with a specific block of narrative, whereas a sea of pages is overwhelming. You can number the scenes, list them, caption them, move them around, and so on. They become manageable.

Likewise, you can box (perhaps using broken lines to indicate partial scenes) those scene segments that are set into narrative passages.

4. Every scene has a *pulse.*

Some vibrancy in the story makes the scene live on the page and makes it matter to the reader. I am calling it a pulse. Sometimes the pulse is subtle and sometimes it beats like a tom-tom, but it is *always* present in a scene. Look for it, dig for it, massage it, burn incense to it if you must. Without it, your scene is a whimper.

I have found in my workshops that writers come up with their own ways of describing this phenomenon, altering it for different kinds of scenes. Here are some of the phrases they have suggested to describe what it is that gives a scene its sine qua non:

An engine	A moment frozen then shattered
A thumping heart	An ember burst into flame;
A question, hanging	or dying
A key turning	A bud that blooms
A stone that causes ripples in	A life force
water	A thrumming
A knot that unravels	A flame of desire

I like all of these—and you can probably come up with descriptions of your own—because they indicate the energy coming from the pulse and driving the scene. Sometimes the nature of the pulse is established in the opening of a scene, in what we call the "setup"* but this is by no means always so.

---

* Where are we? Who is there? What is going on?

Often it simply exists, thrumming beneath the action, causing tension. It may be carried over from an earlier scene; it is something that you, the reader, bring to the scene if the writer has built expectations.

Let me make the subtle distinction between *pulse* and *tension*. which I will discuss more in a later section. Pulse is emotional, an attitude, a state of desire or need. Tension is built from action; it arises from pulse, but it must be created through conflict, whereas pulse is a kind of "steady state," awaiting the trigger to escalate it. So, for example, let's say I want more than anything to be a writer. I neglect other aspects of my life, my relationships, to make time for my writing. I eat fast food and never go to the movies. That ambition is the pulse. Finally there's a big argument (a scene) with my lover, who says if I'm not going to be more available to him, he's going to move out and find someone who is. Now there's tension.

You should be able to state for yourself the pulse of a scene you have written, to be sure that you developed it and were true to it. Read many scenes and articulate the nature of the pulse in each one. On a second pass, ask: Where did awareness of the pulse begin in the story?

Exercises

Write freely without worrying too much about shaping a passage. For now, it is most important to recognize scenes for what they are. You will see that these exercises can be done many times, and you will become better at them.

• *Intersected Scenes:* Reflect on something you have seen that made you curious about what you did not see—"the rest of what happened."

    a. Think of the observed action as a moment near the end of the scene. What might have happened just before?

b. Or think of it as a moment early in the scene. What will happen next? Answering one of these questions will launch a story idea.

• *Memories in Threes:* Reflect on a memory of an event from your life. Think about why the memory stays with you. Perhaps something changed for you afterward. Maybe the incident was unusual and never happened again; or maybe it was so ordinary as to represent a long chain of moments in your life.

a. Tell what happened in three short sentences: a beginning, middle, and end.

b. Then take one of the sentences and write a short paragraph that takes you directly into the place, time, people, and feelings. Moment by moment, tell what happened. You have entered the scene. What is its pulse?

• *Scenes from Photographs:* Choose (or imagine) a photograph of yourself or a photograph of others taken when you were present. Write a scene based on the photo. Be sure that the moment in the photograph is a key moment in the scene. You can write in present or past tense, in first person or third. You could even write in second person ("you"), addressed to someone in the photograph. You could write about the picture:

a. as capturing a single unique event, or

b. as representing "the way things were," such as: "We often took covered dishes down to the river park on summer evenings." Obviously, you can do this exercise many times. Compare the "feel" of the "unique" event in the past, and the "way things were" event (conditional tense). It's the difference between a scene about "the day my mother told me she and my father were divorcing," and one about "the way my dad always walked out of a room, or out of the house, when my mother challenged him about anything he had done."

- **Reactions to Events:** Over a period of a week or so, watch the newspaper for stories about people and events that intrigue you. Make a note of what happened in a brief summary. When you have four or five, come back and, for each one, choose a "moment of entry" into the situation or event. In summary, say what happens next. Then say how the involved person of your choice responded. What did the person do? What might the person have felt (*action/reaction*)? Choose one of the events and write about some part of it, emphasizing the reaction of your chosen person.

  Some examples, from my local newspaper, of events that could be developed into summaries and scenes:

  a. A drunk driver hits a man walking on the shoulder of the road in the fog. What does he do next? (The real event is going to be the driver's decision and action after the accident.)

  b. A famous movie star goes to a refugee camp to serve food for a day, and then flies out in a helicopter. How might one of the refugees respond?

  c. A woman in Oklahoma makes her truant fourteen-year-old daughter stand by the side of the road with a sign that says she is "preparing for her future." Think of the mother's POV (point of view). Think of the daughter's. Think of a girl in a car going by who was just quarreling with her parent.

  d. A prominent man is arrested for child pornography (or embezzlement, etc.). Imagine his wife when he comes home from being booked. (Again, the event is going to emerge from the wife's reaction to her husband's perfidy.)

  e. Two hikers get lost in the woods and are there all night in frigid temperatures before they are rescued. Choose some moment in that time when they become afraid they won't be found and won't survive.

- **Movie Scenes:** List and analyze some scenes from movies that you remember vividly. Ask yourself these questions:

a. What was the action in this scene?
b. What was the emotional response of the characters to the action?
c. What did this scene do for the story? (How was the situation changed by the scene?)
d. What was the pulse of the scene? (That is, what made it feel important; what made it involving?)

• *Movie Summaries:* Choose one movie scene and write a summary, leaving out dialogue and details. Try to get a sense of the scene's structure—the beginning, middle, and end; how did the scene start and end? This exercise is meant to help you build your sense of the elements of scene. It also makes it clear that a summary does not convey story with the same power as scene.

• *Prose Summaries:* Do the same thing you did for movies, except use passages from stories and novels that you have loved.
   Now answer the questions from the beginning of this chapter:
   a. Why are scenes so powerful?
   b. What is a scene?
   c. What are these elements of the scene?
      event
      function
      structure
      pulse

2

EVENT AND MEANING

HOW ACTIONS ADD UP IN SCENES

CONSIDER WHAT IT MEANS TO SAY THAT "SOMETHING HAPPENS" IN A STORY.

- WHAT MAKES ACTION MEANINGFUL?
- HOW DO ACTIONS "ADD UP" IN A SCENE?
- WHAT IS THE DANGER OF ALL TALK IN A SCENE?
- EXERCISES

Significant action

The sum of the overall action of a scene—"what happens"—is the event. Its impact and meaning resonate emotionally for character(s) and for the reader.

Think of the times you have said to someone: Listen, *something happened*. You say this when you are going to tell about a *meaningful event*. Something happens in a scene, too. Something changes or is revealed or new questions are raised; the ground is laid for future events, or the meaning of past events is made clear; characters show themselves to be who they are and make demands on one another. The story is moved along, often through conflict. The protagonist acts and is affected in some way. This happens through decisions and external acts, the stuff of change.

In other words, the things that happen in a scene "add up" to something significant, something with consequences.

When we state what happens on a moment-to-moment level, we are naming the actions. When we state what happens globally, we are naming the event. *Actions + actions = event.* This may seem elementary, but often, apprentice writers get caught up in describing what characters are thinking and feeling, and nothing much happens at all. Or they try to keep the action popping, like a movie, and it's all just a jousting match in which nothing really gets decided or changed. Event does not have to be spectacular, but it does have to be interesting and meaningful. It has to make the story go somewhere. The consequences may be actual and physical—a house burns down, a nose bleeds, a lover moves out of the house—or (and) intellectual and emotional, reverberating beyond the frame of the scene and, ultimately, even the story.

Lively scenes

Let's start by looking at a few scenes where we can really see that *something happens.*

Every scene in "Marie" by Edward P. Jones is marvelous. The story is about an eighty-six-year-old black woman in Washington, D.C., and, among other things, her visit to the Social Security people, who keep summoning her to come and prove she is still entitled to her benefits. As she sets out one morning, she puts a knife in her pocketbook and remembers how, a few weeks before, it saved her life when she went out to buy oatmeal and was accosted by a mugger. In that remembered scene, because she carried no pocketbook, the mugger tried to get into her coat, and he cut his hand on the knife.

"You cut me," he said, as if he had only been minding his own business when she cut him. "Just look what you done to my hand," he said and looked around as if for some witness to her crime. There was not a great amount of blood, but there was enough for her to see it dripping to the pavement. He seemed to be about twenty, no more than twenty-five, dressed the way they were all dressed nowadays, as if a blind man had matched up all their colors. It occurred to her to say that she had seven grand-children his age, that by telling him this he would leave her alone. But the more filth he spoke, the more she wanted him only to come toward her again.

"You done crippled me, you old bitch."

"I sure did," she said, without malice, without triumph, but simply the way she would have told him the time of day had he asked and had she known. She gripped the knife tighter, and as she did, she turned her body ever so slightly so that her good eye lined up with him. Her heart was making an awful racket, wanting to be away from him, wanting to be safe at home. I will not be moved, some organ in the neighborhood of the heart told the heart. "And I got plenty more where that came from."

The last words seemed to bring him down some and, still shaking the blood from his hand, he took a step or two back, which disappointed her. I will not be moved, that other organ kept telling the heart. "You just crazy, thas all," he said. "Just a crazy old hag." Then he turned and lumbered up toward Logan Circle, and several times he looked back over his shoulder as if afraid she might be following. A man came out of Emerson's, then a woman with two little boys. She wanted to grab each of them by the arm and tell them she had come close to losing her life. "I saved myself with this here thing," she would have said. She for-got about the oatmeal and took her raging heart back to the apartment. She told herself that she should, but she never washed the fellow's blood off the knife, and over the next few days it dried and then it began to flake off.

———

The *occasion* for the scene and the *event* are the same: Marie encounters a mugger. Stated in a way that encompasses its meaning, we would say: Marie accidentally overcomes a mugging attempt and is empowered.

There are obviously big things going on in Ron Hansen's story "Wickedness," which compresses numerous horrific events related to a January 1888 Great Plains blizzard into stunning scenes, surveying a number of characters' experiences before expanding the focus on a few. The emotional impact is built through physical action and details. Here is a scene that is so compact it seems like summary until you see that it details specific actions up until the last sentence, which is a single line of summary:

> Ainslie Classen was hopelessly lost in the whiteness and tilting low under the jamming gale when his right elbow jarred against a joist of his pigsty. He walked around the sty by skating his sore red hands along the upright shiplap and then squeezed inside through the slops trough. The pigs scampered over to him, seeking his protection, and Ainslie put himself among them, getting down in their stink and their body heat, socking them away only when they ganged up or when two or three presumed he was food. Hurt was nailing into his finger joints until he thought to work his hands into the pigs' hot wastes, and smeared some onto his skin. The pigs grunted around him and intelligently snuffled at his body with their pink and tender noses, and Ainslie thought, *You are not me but I am you,* and Ainslie Classen got through the night without shame or injury.

The *occasion* for this scene is the blizzard; the *event* is Classen's surviving the night by joining his pigs. There is nothing mysterious about the meaning.

———————

Kate Braverman's scary story "Tall Tales from the Mekong Delta" is about a sicko Vietnam vet, Lenny, who menaces a woman in L.A. and terrifies her (he threatens her young child) into going around with him. There is a scene in which Lenny takes her to swim at a house where the owners are away. He taunts her.

> The water felt strange and icy. It was nothing like she expected. There were shadows on the far side of the pool. The shadows were hideous. There was nothing ambiguous about them. The water beneath the shadows looked remote and troubled and green. It looked contaminated. The more she swam, the more the infected blue particles clustered on her skin. There would be no way to remove them.
>
> "I have to leave," she said.
>
> The sun was going down. It was an unusual sunset for Los Angeles, red and protracted. Clouds formed islands in the red sky. The sprinklers came on. The air smelled damp and green like a forest. There were pine trees beyond the rose garden. She thought of the smell of camp at nightfall, when she was a child.
>
> "What are you? Crazy? You kidding me? I want to take you out," Lenny said. He got out of the pool. He wrapped a towel around his waist. Then he wrapped a towel around her shoulders. "Don't just stand there. Dry off. Come on. You'll get sick. Dry yourself."
>
> He lit a cigarette for her. "You want to get dressed up, right? I know you skinny broads from Beverly Hills. You want to get dressed up. Look. Let me show you something. You'll like it. I know. Come on." He put out his hand for her. She took it . . .

Lenny takes the protagonist swimming illicitly (*occasion*) in someone else's pool, and in doing so increases his menacing hold on her (*event*). The scene conveys that menace not just by what Lenny says but by the flat sentences, as if the woman has lost the courage to assess her surroundings beyond the simplest of descriptions. This scene segues into a more horrific one, in which Lenny takes the woman into a bedroom in the house. "Tales" is a brilliant story, well worth studying for the way a story can be built through the accrual of images and affect.

Often, of course, you can't wholly perceive the meaning of the event if you read the scene out of the context of the story, even if the action is clear. After all, the scene is part of a fabric, not meant to stand alone. Look at this passage from a story of mine, "An Easy Pass," about a day at a Mexican *tienta,* or testing of "brave calves":

> Paolo calls out, This one is last.
>
> It is a little animal, more like a goat than a cow, with imma-
> ture horns and a furious twitchy tail. I grab Chule's cape and run
> into the ring, almost meeting Marcelo in the middle. He passes
> the calf and hisses at me to get out. There is a minor clamor, but
> I hear Paolo say, It's well enough.
>
> Chule has played the cow on the other side of the ring, and
> Marcelo, probably in disgust, has turned his back behind the
> boards. The little cow tosses her head and turns, looking this way
> and that. Behind me, I hear Leon call, Go toward the center, and
> I do. I hold the cape out and high, as if it were Chule coming
> toward me. The cow sees the lure and comes for it. I don't have
> time to be afraid, though I will remember those moments after-
> wards in slow motion, as if I had all the time in the world to turn
> and run.
>
> I am lucky. The cow is a good girl, straight and fast, thoroughly
> annoyed, and not afraid. She behaves the way she is meant to be-
> have, and that makes my simple pass the right one to let her by.
> As I lift my cape behind her, I know my pass has not been beau-
> tiful, but look at me: I stand my ground and look into the stands
> for Paolo, finding only the glare of the sun.
>
> The animal skids to a stop behind me, looks around, and de-
> cides to charge again. I know this because this is what a good

calf does in the ring in a *tienta*. It is my place to turn, too, and to pass her again, but I am still, as if my clock has stopped. Someone calls out to me and I turn quickly and hold out the cape again.

She slips by me so close I see the ridge of her back. She runs toward the barrier where Leonardo and Chule are calling to her. I drop the cape to the ground. I hear the matador Lara call out, in clear English, Now run! and I do, while behind me the young men work the cow to an exit.

I ride back in a jeep with Leonardo, Chule, Rosie and the actress. They clap me on the back and tell me I am a brave chihuahua. I go straight to the bunkhouse and lock myself in my room. Nobody comes for me for dinner. I am afraid I have embarrassed Paolo and myself. Suddenly I ache with exhaustion, and I go to bed.

This scene occurs late in the story that has established the narrator's position in the household of the rancher and matador Paolo. Our best clue to the meaning of the scene is in the moment when she looks to him after her simple pass, saying, "I stand my ground and look into the stands for Paolo, finding only the glare of the sun." We have to wait to see how he reacts to her little show. Here is what we have, listed in these steps of analysis: summary, beats of action, compression into event, emotion.

  a. *Summary:* A young woman seizes the opportunity to go into the practice ring at a *tienta,* where she capes a small calf as her lover and others look on. After two passes, she gives up and leaves the ring.

  b. *Actions:* She grabs the cape and enters the ring. Marcelo passes the calf and tells the girl to leave the ring, but she doesn't. She goes to the center of the ring, holds up her cape, and passes the calf. She passes the calf again, then drops the cape and runs to the exit. (The last paragraph is a summary of the follow-up.)

c. *Event:* A young woman sneaks into the ring and passes a little calf in order to impress her lover.

d. *Emotion:* There is a pulse in the scene driving her to this bit of bravado—she wants her lover to approve. She shows little affect, as if her performance is meaningless. Perhaps more will be explained in the later narrative.

Sometimes the event is subtle though deeply resonant. In Stuart Dybek's "Pet Milk," the narrator recalls a lost love, a girl he went with in Chicago briefly after college, before he went to Europe. He says that as they talked about their plans for the future, it was "the first tme I'd ever had the feeling of missing someone I was still with." In the last scene of the story, the couple gets on the train and necks all the way home to Evanston. He describes the rocking of the train and the landscape they speed past. He describes the faces of passengers waiting on a platform as the express rushes by a local station. The event of this scene is straightforward: A couple makes out while traveling the El home one evening. Note how the narrator pulls the meaning from it in his reflection on one moment of that day. If I were marking this for <u>event</u> and [meaning] (response), I might use my underlines and brackets as follows:

. . . A high school kid in shirt sleeves, maybe sixteen, with books tucked under one arm and a cigarette in his mouth, caught sight of us, and in the instant before he disappeared <u>he grinned and started to wave</u>. Then he was gone, and <u>I turned</u> from the window, back to Kate, [forgetting everything—the passing stations, the glowing late sky, even the sense of missing her—but that arrested wave stayed with me. It was as if I were standing on that platform, with my schoolbooks and a smoke, on one of those endlessly accumulated afternoons after school when I stood almost outside of time simply waiting for a train, and I thought how much I'd have loved seeing someone like us streaming by].

The strength of Dybek's story is in the telling: The actions are simple, but they are thick with meaning because the narrator tells them from a long view, that is, he conflates action and reaction in the scene.

Dialogue: Feeling arises from experience

This is true for your characters and this is true for your readers. It's a tricky thing to make dialogue work as experience.

Say, for example, that you have a friend come to the apartment of your character, Phoebe, where they talk about Phoebe's suspicions that her boyfriend is running around on her. There is a lot of dialogue, and maybe, if you remember to ground the scene in actions, you have the friends do something, like fold laundry or rearrange furniture. It will seem that there is *activity,* but what is the *event?*

If they just go round and round, the scene goes nowhere. If the scene works, the event has to be something more than "Two friends talk about their suspicions," which is the sum of the action. (Their background movement is just that, movement, not action, because it does not make anything happen or change.)

Suppose that in the course of the scene Phoebe follows her suspicions and probes her friend, growing more and more aggressive, until the friend finally admits that she is Phoebe's boyfriend's lover. Now we do have an event arising from the dialogue: "Phoebe discovers her friend's betrayal." Discovery is the true sum of the action—the outcome of the dialogue.

I raised the problem of a scene that is all talk because so many apprentice scenes are written like this, often with a lot of interior musing, too, and it can be difficult for the author to understand why a reader's reaction is that nothing seems to be happening in the scene. What you must remember with such passages is that dialogue has to add up to something. It has to light a fire.

———————

Let's look at an example of a dialogue-driven event, one in which two characters are just sitting and talking—and something does happen. The event is a *decision*.

In the novel *Love Among the Ruins*, by Robert Clark, a high school couple, Emily and William, have become romantically involved over a summer. William is a little older than Emily and recklessly intense, mostly because it is the sixties and his mother is radical and he's facing the draft. He's convinced himself that he has to run away and live in the wilderness, and he's worked on convincing Emily to come with him—all through talk. In a short, pivotal scene, he reads something in the newspaper to her about "the system and the draft and everything," and he pushes her to say that things are falling apart, that they have only each other. For all practical purposes, he has been indoctrinating her (believing fully that he is right), and it is in this moment that she acquiesces:

The next afternoon, Friday, in the apartment, William and Emily made love and looked at the newspaper, and he said to her, "So now do you see? About the system and the draft and everything?" He did not intend this to sound mean—he was merely in the grip of an intention, a new one undergirded by fear and panic—but it sounded cruel to Emily. It could almost have undone all that they had become to each other, except that the past five days had been perfect, and everything outside of them had been shown to be evil and false; and that, or at least the contrast between the two of them and the world, Emily understood with complete clarity.

"I see. And I didn't ever not believe you. Not ever," she said.

William felt the awful paltriness of his faith, his ingratitude and blindness, and the forgiveness Emily's response contained. "I know. I don't know why I said that. I guess I'm scared."

"I'm scared too."

"So what do you do?"

"I'm not sure. I'm not you."

William said, "Yes you are. We're each other now, even if everything else falls apart. Right?"

Emily said, "Right." She said this not in acquiescence, but as a statement of fact, of what she believed entirely.

William went on. "So you be me. Tell me what we think."

Emily paused, and then she licked her lips and spoke. She told him that all our life is some form of religion, and all our action some belief. In his case, she thought he was called upon to do his duty to himself, that is, to God in the end.[*]

William asked, "Are you going with me?"

And Emily said, "I suppose I am."

The *occasion* for this scene is the couple's meeting in the apartment. And what is the *event*? William convinces Emily to run away with him. The actions consist of his argument and then the responses of both of them—he reviewing his own fears; she expressing hers but then embracing his argument, going beyond it to make it something holy, and then agreeing to go. How brilliantly William argues when he transfers the weight of the decision to Emily!

So it is that these two young people head off into the wilderness toward tragedy. Emily's fear is palpable as she yields to the seduction of William's romantic terrorizing, but there is also a sense of release.

Young British tourist Lucy Honeychurch visits passionate Italy with her stingy-minded chaperone, Charlotte Bartlett, in E. M. Forster's charming *A Room with a View,* a novel full of memorable scenes driven by delightful dialogue.[†] As soon as the women arrive at their pensione, they meet the Emersons, father and son.

---

[*] Note that this paragraph summarizing what Emily said is *indirect dialogue.* The author's strategy is to compress this very dramatic talk, which might have taken a page or more in dialogue, so that the utter simplicity of the last two sentences is stark. It is quite effective.

[†] Both Signet Classics and Barnes & Noble have inexpensive paperbacks with introductions available.

The younger is melancholic George, an unsuitable young man who grows more and more attractive to Lucy, a girl who has a hard time knowing her own mind. Soon after, they encounter each other in a piazza where Lucy has just witnessed the fatal stabbing of an Italian. She faints, and George, who happened to be nearby, comes to her aid. She sends him to fetch her dropped photographs and then insists she is fit to walk home alone. He insists that she is not, gets his way, and they proceed toward the Arno, talking of the murder. Then:

"... What was that?"

He had thrown something into the stream.

"What did you throw in?"

"Things I didn't want," he said crossly.

"Mr. Emerson!"

"Well?"

"Where are the photographs?"

He was silent.

"I believe it was my photographs that you threw away."

"I didn't know what to do with them," he cried, and his voice was that of an anxious boy. Her heart warmed towards him for the first time. "They were covered with blood. There! I'm glad I've told you; and all the time we were making conversation I was wondering what to do with them." He pointed down-stream. "They've gone." The river swirled under the bridge. "I did mind them so, and one is so foolish, it seemed better that they should go out to the sea—I don't know; I may just mean that they frightened me." Then the boy verged into a man. "For something tremendous has happened; I must face it without getting muddled. It isn't exactly that a man has died."

Something warned Lucy that she must stop him.

"It has happened," he repeated, "and I mean to find out what it is."

"Mr. Emerson—"

He turned towards her frowning, as if she had disturbed him in some abstract quest.

"I want to ask you something before we go in."

They were close to their pension. She stopped and leant her elbows against the parapet of the embankment. He did likewise. There is at times a magic in identity of position; it is one of the things that have suggested to us eternal comradeship. She moved her elbows before saying:

"I have behaved ridiculously."

He was following his own thoughts.

"I was never so much ashamed of myself in my life; I cannot think what came over me."

"I nearly fainted myself," he said; but she felt that her attitude repelled him.

"Well, I owe you a thousand apologies."

"Oh, all right."

"And—this is the real point—you know how silly people are gossiping—ladies especially, I am afraid—you understand what I mean?"

"I'm afraid I don't."

"I mean, would you not mention it to anyone, my foolish behaviour?"

"Your behaviour? Oh, yes, all right—all right."

"Thank you so much. And would you—"

She could not carry her request any further. The river was rushing below them, almost black in the advancing night. He had thrown her photographs into it, and then he had told her the reason. It struck her that it was hopeless to look for chivalry in such a man. He would do her no harm by idle gossip; he was trustworthy, intelligent, and even kind; he might even have a high opinion of her. But he lacked chivalry; his thoughts, like his behaviour, would not be modified by awe. It was useless to say to him, "And would you—" and hope that he would complete the sentence for himself, averting his eyes from her nakedness like the knight in that beautiful picture. She had been in his arms, and he remembered it, just as he remembered the blood on the photographs that she had bought in Alinari's shop. It was not exactly that a man had died; something had happened to the living: they had come to a situation where character tells, and where Childhood enters upon the branching paths of Youth.

"Well, thank you so much," she repeated. "How quickly these accidents do happen, and then one returns to the old life!"

"I don't."

Anxiety moved her to question him.

His answer was puzzling: "I shall probably want to live."

"But why, Mr. Emerson? What do you mean?"

"I shall want to live, I say."

Leaning her elbows on the parapet, she contemplated the River Arno, whose roar was suggesting some unexpected melody to her ears.

Keep in mind that each of Mr. Forster's chapters is quite like a story, or certainly a full episode in his narrative. I have taken the latter portion of this particular episode, after the murder in the piazza that led to the meeting of Lucy and George, all of which set up the possibility of this first real conversation between them. So much "happens" in the dialogue! Their stodgy world begins to open to possibilities of friendship between them. We see their characters: Lucy, with her worries about propriety that have been so thoroughly drilled into her; George, still a mystery, with his allusion to desiring life. The important thing is that they have had a chance to speak at all, alone and with some honesty. In her reflection, Lucy seems to sum up George, but his last statement surprises her and gives the reader something to ponder, too. Clever Forster.

In Frank Conroy's classic collection of stories, *Midair*, the title story is about a man, Sean, divorced, who one day is caught for a few moments in an elevator that stops between floors. By that time we know quite a lot about him, including a memory that is narrated in the opening passage, set in 1942, when his father is more or less dragging Sean, age six, and his sister, Mary, age nine, along the Lower East Side of New York to their apartment. He has to break in by way of the fire escape. The children are baffled by his presence. An hour later we catch up with them as they are rearranging books alphabetically by author, then cleaning windows. The children, waiting for their mother to come home from work, are growing afraid. Finally people come for the father, who is obviously quite ill. Following is the end of the scene and of the 1942 passage, before the story jumps forward in time to Sean's adulthood.

A tremendous crash as the door is kicked in, the frame splintering where the chain has come away. Sean is aware that things are happening very fast now, and yet he can see it all with remarkable clarity. Wood chips drift lazily through the air. Three men rush through the door—two in white uniforms, one in ordinary clothes. He knows they are running toward the couch as fast as they can—their faces frozen masks of strain—but time itself seems to have slowed down.

Still clamped to his father's side, Sean feels himself rise up into the air. He sees his father's other hand make a grab for Mary, who is trying to escape. He gets hold of her hair, but she twists away with a yell. Sean feels betrayed that she has gotten away. She was the one calling him Daddy. The wind roars as the big man rushes to the window and climbs out on the sill.

"Stop where you are!" he shouts back at the men.

Sean cannot see, but he senses that the men have stopped. He can hear Mary crying, hear the wind, and hear the sound of his father's heart racing under the rough tweed of his jacket. He stares down at the street, at the cracks in the sidewalk. With the very limited motion available to his arms, he finds his father's belt and hangs on with both fists.

"You bastards," his father shouts. "What you don't realize is that I can do anything. Anything!"

Something akin to sleepiness comes over Sean. As time passes he realizes—a message from a distant outpost—that he has soiled himself. Finally, they are pulled back in, with great speed and strength, and fall to the floor. His father screams as the men cover him.

I close with this example because it is truly a large event: An imbalanced man climbs onto a windowsill using his own son as hostage against intruders. The mere statement of what happens carries the feeling. Read the story to see how Conroy enlarges the meaning of the passage in the context of Sean's life.

Exercises

• **Reading for Event:** Read stories and passages from books. Identify scenes* and read each one several times. Then state
  a. the occasion for the scene (why these characters are together),
  b. the event of the scene, and
  c. the emotion built in the scene.

It may be helpful to you to start by simply summarizing the scene, then compressing that even more, into an overall statement. It is worth every minute of your time to go through this process:

> read
>
> summarize
>
> compress

You will know you are on the right track if your summary statement is an umbrella under which you can list the actions of the scene that add up to the event—and if it takes all those actions in order for the emotion to develop and be conveyed.

This is excellent work for a writing group, in which members bring in favorite scenes to share and analyze. Avoid very complex prose. Look for scenes that are clear to you. You'll have time enough to complicate things later!

---

* Remember that some scenes will be embedded in passages of narrative summary; look for the points where the narrative slows down and goes into the moment.

Here are some writers who could serve you well, because they use scenes copiously, and I think you will be able to easily find ones that you like and can block out for study. They vary in complexity and style. If you are interested in young-adult fiction, ask your librarian or bookstore owner for recommendations of award-winning novels to find well-crafted models. There are many good ones, and in their relative simplicity they are excellent studies.

Hint: It helps if you <u>underline the actions</u> in your selected scene.

Sherman Alexie
A. Manette Ansay
Margaret Atwood
  (see *Bodily Harm*
  and *Life Before Man*)
Elizabeth Berg
Tracy Chevalier
Michael Connelly
Chitra Banerjee
  Divakaruni
Tim Farrington
Fannie Flagg
Karen Joy Fowler
Elizabeth George
Beth Gutcheon

Jane Hamilton
Joanne Harris
Kent Haruf
Jon Hassler
Ann Hood
Pam Houston
Francisco Jiménez
Ha Jin
Diane Johnson
Heidi Julavits
David Michael Kaplan
John le Carré
Beth Lordan
Erin McGraw
Henning Mankell

Haruki Murakami
Gina Ochsner
Julie Orringer
Ann Patchett
Susan Power
Anna Quindlen
Sheri Reynolds
Roxana Robinson
Annette Sanford
Katherine Shonk
Jean Thompson
Kathleen Tyau
Anne Tyler
Larry Watson
Monica Wood

In my own work, you will find that the novels *More Than Allies, Opal on Dry Ground, A Chance to See Egypt,* and *Beyond Deserving,* named in ascending order of structural complexity, are built almost entirely of scenes.

• **Compiling Events:** Keep a running list of ideas for occasions that can lead to scene events. Don't worry about the whole story at this point. The idea is to practice conceiving a unit of narrative that has enough action and meaning to suggest a strong scene. You are looking for moments when things are off-kilter in some way. Look for situations when a character is under stress. What might happen next?

Here are some sample situations:

a. A young teenager creeps into her dark house and finds her parents waiting for her. (Will this be a scene of defiance and authority, or perhaps one of worry and contrition? Ah, perhaps false contrition and promises about the future?)

b. A man slips into a swimming pool unnoticed and moves toward a woman floating on an inner tube in the deep end. (Scary? Or seductive?)

c. A woman comes home from a trip to discover her house is full of pests (bats, raccoons, rats, teenagers?).

d. Children are streaming from an elementary school, shouting and crying.

e. An adult child arrives home to the bedside of a dying, estranged parent.

f. An obese young woman steps onto a scale while her friend stands by her, waiting to write down her weight.

g. High above the beach, a tourist looks down and sees a woman flailing in the surf.

Pay attention to the kinds of decisions you have to make in order to go on from this point: Who will the story be about? Where and when will you start the action? Who is in the scene? Most of all, what will the event be?

Many writers have reported that their stories, or even novels, have begun with nothing more than such an image or idea.

• *The Cheat Sheet:* Choose three stories you have read fairly recently and liked. For each one:

a. List the first event of the story: What happens? What is set in motion? Don't list too many details.

   b. Do this for each story. Now set your notes aside for a week
   or more.
   c. Come back to your notes. Read your description of an
   event—but not the original story. Make up your own version of the same event, changing the circumstances significantly, or as you like. What is the action? What is the
   emotional response? (You will probably find yourself in entirely new territory. At worst, you will write some ghost
   version of the original, and practice scene writing.)

• ***The Theme Corral:*** Frank O'Connor said that when someone
told him a good story, he made a note of four lines, thereby capturing the theme or idea of the story, and not committing himself to characters, setting, etc. Try his approach. Record the
essence of a told story—what it is "about"—without worrying
about any details, maybe not even the event. Just what it seems
to "add up to." As in the preceding exercise, set your notes aside
and come back to them at a later time. See what kind of scene
or story comes to mind from your brief record of the original
stimulus. (The more times you do this, the better it will work
for you.)
   Examples:
   a. A weak man is challenged in a life-and-death situation and
   discovers unknown strengths within himself. He finds the
   courage to put others' needs before his own, and the wits
   to create a strategy to escape danger.
   b. Everything falls apart in one day for a woman who discovers her life really is back at square one. At first she
   blames circumstances and other people; she rails against her
   bad luck and the disloyalty of friends, but she's not weak,
   just damaged and foolish. She can start over.
   c. A woman who has made her living taking care of old and
   dying people in a rest home finds herself with what she
   considers an impossible situation: Her mother is dying.
   Nothing she knows that is practical seems relevant and her

religious life seems vapid. She has to learn from her mother how to allow her to die.

Now think over what you have learned in this chapter and in these exercises. Articulate what you have learned.

- What makes action meaningful? What does it mean to say that "something happens" in a scene?
- How do actions "add up" in a scene?
- What is the danger of all talk in a scene? How can you "test" your scene to see if you have avoided this trap?

3
BEATS

HOW A STRONG CENTRAL EVENT CAN BE BROKEN DOWN INTO BEATS

- WHAT ARE BEATS?
- HOW ARE THEY USED IN PLANNING AND REVISING SCENES?
- EXERCISES

Steps of action

Beats are small units of character action and reaction.

I'm always gratified by how helpful the concepts of *event* and *beats* are in getting apprentice writers to construct strong scenes. In the course of a one-day workshop I often see big jumps in the quality of ideas for scenes after these concepts are used to strengthen focus and structure. I'm sure you will have the same experience.

The term *beats* refers to the way one breaks down events into small steps of action, making it possible to evaluate whether those steps move the action effectively toward the culmination of the scene. Even if the beats are nested in a scene dense with description or reflection, making them clear and vivid will keep the line of action in the reader's mind as the scene moves toward the outcome of the event. If the beats are weakly written, they will be lost in such a scene. In a high-action scene, having the beats clearly thought out makes it easier to control the pacing. Reviewing the beats in a scene also helps you review the logic of the scene, to see if you have included all the steps you need to make the action plausible.

The best way to illustrate the idea is with a scene, of course. We meet up with Lucy and George again in *A Room with a View*. Lucy has been in the country for the afternoon with several elderly companions. The older ladies are tired and ready to return to Florence. Lucy wants to search for the clergymen who should take them; they have wandered off on foot. She asks one of the waiting carriage drivers to take her to find them. It must be a relief to Lucy to go off like this, away from the old people, even if it is to find more old people! She loves the countryside and the chance to think about where she is. Watch for the beats of the walk and then the great shift in the energy of the scene as there is a change not only in the setting but in the person she finds there. And then the terrible interruption.

He only stopped once, to pick her some great blue violets. She thanked him with real pleasure. In the company of this common man the world was beautiful and direct. For the first time she felt the influence of Spring. His arm swept the horizon gracefully; violets, like other things, existed in great profusion there; would she like to see them?

"Ma buoni uomini."

He bowed. Certainly. Good men first, violets afterwards. They proceeded briskly through the undergrowth, which became thicker and thicker. They were nearing the edge of the promontory, and the view was stealing round them, but the brown network of the bushes shattered it into countless pieces. He was occupied in his cigar, and in holding back the pliant boughs. She was rejoicing in her escape from dullness. Not a step, not a twig, was unimportant to her.

"What is that?"

There was a voice in the wood, in the distance behind them. The voice of Mr. Eager? He shrugged his shoulders. An Italian's ignorance is sometimes more remarkable than his knowledge. She could not make him understand that perhaps they had missed the clergymen. The view was forming at last; she could discern the river, the golden plain, other hills.

"Eccolo!" he exclaimed.

At the same moment the ground gave way, and with a cry she fell out of the wood. Light and beauty enveloped her. She had fallen onto a little open terrace, which was covered with violets from end to end.

"Courage!" cried her companion, now standing some six feet above. "Courage and love."

She did not answer. From her feet the ground sloped sharply into view, and violets ran down in rivulets and streams and cataracts, irrigating the hillside with blue, eddying round the tree stems, collecting into pools in the hollows, covering the grass with spots of azure foam. But never again were they in such profusion; this terrace was the well-head, the primal source whence beauty gushed out to water the earth.

Standing at its brink, like a swimmer who prepares, was the good man. But he was not the good man that she had expected, and he was alone.

George had turned at the sound of her arrival. For a moment he contemplated her, as one who had fallen out of heaven. He saw radiant joy in her face, he saw the flowers beat against her dress in blue waves. The bushes above them closed. He stepped quickly forward and kissed her.

Before she could speak, almost before she could feel, a voice called, "Lucy! Lucy! Lucy!" The silence of life had been broken by Miss Bartlett, who stood brown against the view.

Many things happen in this brief scene, though the scene is also profuse with the beauty of its setting, which is so necessary to what happens. See how the author paints the rich portrait of the place and of Lucy's happiness in this sublime countryside, while clearly choreographing the beats of action:

- The driver stops to pick Lucy some flowers.
- She hears a voice in the wood.

- The driver cries out, "There he is!"
- She runs onto a little open terrace as her companion calls to her.
- George steps toward her. (His other actions are before this, simultaneous with her movements: his turn at the sound of her arrival, etc.)
- He kisses her.
- Miss Bartlett calls her name. (And don't you want to throttle her?)

The following gently paced scene is from "Daughter of the Moon" by Janet Peery. You need to know that a family has lost its young mother to death, and both grandmothers are now in the house helping the young father look after his children. The maternal grandmother, who is called Pye Tee, is having the hardest time, especially since the other grandmother thinks that Pye Tee shouldn't talk about the dead woman, who is Pye Tee's own daughter. Pye Tee is starting to do foolish things unwittingly, like wet her pants, and all she can think to do is make a space that feels safe to her.

Roy is her little grandson.

The next morning, Pye Tee took Roy with her to the garage, where she rummaged for the camping tent. She worked most of the morning to set it up beneath the black walnut tree in the back yard, wrestling with the flimsy threaded poles and maroon material. When she had finished, she stood off a ways to inspect her work. Fine, it looked, inviting; a dusky red dome, crisscross poles like spines of a great deep basket, overturned. When she saw Big Nana watching from the kitchen window, Pye Tee waved gaily. Inside the tent, the air was warm and musty. Roy crawled in beside her. "Pye Tee's house," he said. He lay down on the quilt she'd spread.

"The wigwam of Nokomis," said Pye Tee, remembering the Hiawatha poem. "Daughter of the Moon, Nokomis."

Dreamily, Roy waved his hands above his face. "Red air."

"Yes," Pye Tee agreed. She lay back beside him. The ground seemed to rise up to hold her, and in the moment just before she fell asleep, she was visited by the sense that she was holding something off.

Glancing over the description, note the beats:

Pye Tee takes Roy in the garage
and she rummages for the tent,
works to set it up
and inspects her work.
She sees Big Nana and waves to her.
She crawls in with Roy
and Roy lies down.
She and Roy exchange comments about a character from *The Song of Hiawatha*
and she lies back.

It is instructive, then, to look again and see how the descriptions of objects and feelings go along with the beats of action. It's a beautiful interweaving of character interaction, theme, and mood, but all those things work because Pye Tee is *doing something;* she is establishing a kind of King's X for her and her grandchildren.

The following scene is taken from the fine novel *The Underpainter* by Canadian novelist Jane Urquhart. The book is painterly and passionate; it has been described as being about "the geography of imagination." Yet even in such a diffused narrative, the author is careful to give the reader relevant description and small action beats that help put reflection in *place;* a real person is thinking, and that person is somewhere, doing something, even alone. (Within the brackets, you can see the beats of action.)

She is standing near the window beside a rough log wall. The unopened telegram in her hand appears to have already darkened with time, darkened in comparison to the white snow around her house, the brightness of sun that enters the room.

[She pushes a tendril of hair behind her ear, a strand that has escaped the braid.] This strand contains some threads of grey. [She stares at the envelope, then lifts her head to watch the departure of the mail sled, its driver and team of noisy dogs, to watch it glide over the snow-covered ice and disappear behind Burnt Island.] For several minutes she wants to refuse the message she has not yet read. The world around her is quiet and fixed, frozen and beautiful. She does not want the scene disturbed. Even the tracks of the sled irritate her; they have scarred the white surface, they have soiled the day. *(Here there is a paragraph about the winters, "long and bright and silent.")*

[She crosses the room and lifts the lid of the Quebec heater, which she holds at the end of the lever for some time as if not quite certain why she has taken this action.] For a moment it looks as if she will toss the telegram, unread, into the fire. But this is not what she wants. [When she replaces the lid,] there is the sound of cast iron striking cast iron, a sound so familiar to her she barely hears it.

Sitting on the chair near the stove's heat, [she carefully opens the envelope. It falls to her lap. She reads the contents.]

The central event of the scene is her reading of the letter, an act she does not come to easily. The rest of the passage is made up of description and *interiority,* that is, the thoughts of the character. Thus, the reaction is emotional rather than active.

The scenes that I am using as models are from longer works, but in fact a scene can be a very short story in itself, even so complete that it can stand alone. One of my favorite examples is Lydia Davis's "The Outing," from her collection *Almost No Memory.* Her story is a series of noun phrases that add up, almost like a poem, to a story. The story is a single continuous scene. Although there is no dialogue, indeed no verbs, there is a clear progression of both event and emotion, spelled out in *beats.*

An outburst of anger near the road, a refusal to speak on the path, a silence in the pine woods, a silence across the old railroad bridge, an attempt to be friendly in the water, a refusal to end the argument on the flat stones, a cry of anger on the steep bank of dirt, a weeping among the bushes.

In eight phrases we are moved from a consideration of a quarrel to its end and the emotional fallout from it. (Note that we don't know what the quarrel was about; it doesn't really matter.) We see the stages along the way, in which it does not seem to be possible to make things right. The inconclusiveness is the very engine of the story, and Davis scrutinizes it in a way that leaves us having experienced a dramatic scene even though we don't know what the conflict is about. The story isn't about the conflict; it is about its dying moments, when the characters cannot resolve it. "The Outing" is a truly original story because it works outside our usual notions about what a story is. Yet I am able to find in it a model of narrative structure, the beat.

Without taking anything from Davis's accomplishment (I admire her work enormously), I use this model as the main focus of my attention on her story. When you examine the story beat by beat, think of it as an outline, as if you intended to write conventional prose. It might help you to understand the structure of the story if you lay the phrases out on separate lines, then study them carefully. You will see that the lines are paired in action and reaction: The "outburst" is met with a "refusal"; "silence" with "silence"; and so on, until, at the end, there is "weeping." Trying to understand what happens creates the story in your mind. (I suspect that if you do this with a friend, you'll find that your interpretations differ.)

Remember when I mentioned waiting at a light and seeing a man throw a box into a car, slam the trunk, and speed away? Let's use that in order to build an example of a beat list for a scene. In this case, I am going to demonstrate the difference when the scene is looked at from *outside* the event versus *inside* the event.

Here is my first scene beat list:

<u>A man throws a box</u> in a car in a driveway while a woman
    watches. (Children stand farther back, near the house.)
<u>The car pulls away</u> and <u>the woman chases</u> the car, screaming.
<u>Another woman</u> along the shoulder of the road calls out and
    <u>the first woman goes</u> to her; <u>they embrace</u>.
<u>Children,</u> huddled in the driveway, <u>whimper</u>.

As the author, I am thinking that the event was the departure
of the father. At the beginning, the children are in the background, not a part of the first beats. I see the scene closing on the
children, leaning on one another, waiting for their mother to
gather her wits and come back to them. I conceive of the scene
as conveyed by a narrator who is not part of the story. In this
strategy, I would describe what happens objectively, expecting the
weight of the actions to carry the sorrow in them.

If, on the other hand, I wanted to use the woman's point of
view (POV), my beat list might look like this:

<u>He slams the hatch</u> closed and <u>looks at the children</u> but not at me.
<u>He drives away</u>
and <u>I run after</u> him.
My <u>sister calls</u> to me,
<u>I see him go</u> through the intersection,
and <u>I go to her</u> on the shoulder of the road.
<u>We turn</u> to go back
and <u>I see the kids</u> looking like refugees from a catastrophic
    storm;
(now an emotional beat) I realize that I had not been think-
    ing of them.

Notice that in the second instance, which is from the mother's
point of view, the narrator has not expressed feelings, although
they underlie the beats of action, until the end, when she says that

she had forgotten her children, a statement that carries the weight
of her feeling for them.

Vocabulary

inciting event: the action that "gets things going"

state of things: the way things are; the circumstances surrounding an event or the resolution of an event

observed motion and *felt motion:* distinguishes between what a
character sees and what a character experiences directly

grounding a scene: the ways that the author gives the scene a
sense of place and time and circumstance through small actions, objects, and senses

shift in action: a turn in the progression of the event; something
small or large that makes a difference in how things may
turn out; a change in circumstances

interiority: the things that the character thinks, whether in direct response to the actions of the scene or with tangents
such as flashbacks

close POV: the telling of events from a particular character's actions and intimate thoughts

Exercises

• *Two Views of an Emotional Event:* Think of an event that has
emotional repercussions (i.e., an *inciting event*), and then list the
steps (beats) of what occurs from after the inciting event to the
closing *state of things* (how things are at the end). Feel free to vary
the grammatical constructions; use sentences if you want to. Try
it various ways. If you spend the time doing this twice, you will
learn about the difference between *observed* motion and *felt* emotion when it is conveyed by the writer. Plan:

    a. a scene written from outside the event, as by an observer
or detached narrator;

b. a scene written from inside the event, with a close POV, whether first or third person.

The structure of this scene: situation/line of actions/new situation.

• *Boxed Scenes:* Take a story of yours. Using a broad-tipped marker or crayon, "box in" your scenes, clearly demarcating where they begin and end. Then, on a separate sheet of paper, make a title or caption for each scene and list the beats of action. Ask yourself:

a. Is it clear where a scene begins and ends?

b. Is it clear where it takes place and how much time it covers? Do we have a sense of "being there"?

c. Does something clearly happen? Can I summarize it in a sentence?

d. Is there some change in the way things are for the protagonist as a result of the action (a "shift")?

Obviously, if the answer to any of these questions is no, you have work to do!

• *A Mission:* Think of an urgent mission for a character, something that must be accomplished in a close time frame, and put the character into early pursuit of the goal. Cover only a few moments in your scene, and make the beats of action escalate the sense of urgency. Leave your character at a point of frustration. Try envisioning this occurring inside a building; try it outside in an open landscape. Try it with other people around to provide obstacles. Another time, the setting can provide the obstacles.

• *Reading for Beats:* What these examples have illustrated is that a scene is composed of *beats:* units of progression through an event, i.e., through action. Look at a story you admire and pick a scene. Be sure you know when the scene begins and ends. Then identify each beat of the scene. Write a sentence or phrase to represent the action. The sum of those beats is the scene.

Repeat with many other scenes and stories. Choose scenes that move right along (Elmore Leonard, Edwidge Danticat, Kent Haruf, Jhumpa Lahiri in *Interpreter of Maladies*, etc.), and then work with writers who write dense, textured prose (Rohintin Mistry, Richard Russo, Sue Miller, V. S. Naipaul, William Trevor, Robert Clark, Alice Munro, Charles Baxter, Ann Patchett, etc.). This must become second nature to you!

Study the way a mystery writer uses beats. Generally, mystery writers write mostly in scenes and use longer scenes, especially the Brits. Often, the scenes impart a great deal of information, so the author has to create a situation where the investigator is interacting with someone so that the scene isn't static. If there's some kind of spark, good or bad, between people in the scene, it livens up what is essentially exposition.

• **Procrastination:** Write a brief scene in which a character has to do something he doesn't want to do: make a call, read a letter, leave the house. Think of action that will indicate that the character has embarked on the procrastinated action (that is the "end point" of your scene); then write a sequence of avoidance steps up to that point, and "dress" the scene with description and the character's thoughts.

• **Cleaning Up Mud:** Study one of your scenes that feels "muddy" or "floating." List the beats of action that you have written or that you meant to write. *Repairing the beats will give you a revision outline.* If you see that the action is not clear, make it so. Sometimes the fuzziness comes from failure to put the scene firmly into place ("grounding") through concrete details. Perhaps we don't know where we are in space or time. You want to make the scene both tighter and more specific. Then you can make the beats escalate in tension. This is how emotion is built. If the action beats of the scene create tension, then you can look at the scene to see what the responses of the characters are. It is possible to make a list of *emotion beats,* the ways that characters react to specific actions. Remember, though, that feelings are not actions. They become action when they are translated into something physical, when someone does something. Look at the response beats and answer these questions:

   a. Which emotional beats are *reactions* to actions?
   b. Which emotional beats *result* in actions?
   c. Are emotions expressed in dialogue or action or both?
   d. Are some emotions hidden? Why?
   e. When are the emotions expressed in *interiority,* that is, the unspoken musing of the POV character?

Examine your scene again so that you see the relationship of actions and emotions.

If you are intimidated by this extension of the exercise at this time, attach a Post-it note or a paper clip to the page and come back to it later, when you feel more confident about your control of action beats. Try lining up action and emotion beats by analyzing a published scene before you tackle your own writing.

The more you read for beats, write beats in outline, and identify beats in your drafts, the easier all this will become, until it is second nature and you hardly have to think about them at all until you are revising and you want to look at the manuscript analytically.

Review what you now know about beats.
   • What are beats?
   • Give some examples of ways they are used to plan or evaluate scenes.

4

THE FOCAL POINT

A PLACE WHERE A SCENE CONVERGES
AND TURNS

FIND THE PLACE WHERE THE SCENE TURNS.

■ CAN YOU PUT YOUR FINGER ON A SCENE'S HOT SPOT?

You know one when you've got it

You decide what to call it. Nugget. Moment. Apex. Focal
point. Turn. Tip. Hot spot.

If you don't have one, the scene is boring. Think about where
the scene's essence lies: the point at which everything changes.
There is Before X and After X. X is the focal point.

Sometimes it comes early, because you don't always spend
time on the beginning of the scene; you just launch it. Sometimes
it comes late, because there's a long buildup to the event. But
you'll sense that there's momentum both before and after X.
There's movement *away from something* or *toward something*. Because you wrote the moment of X, you can't go backward. You
can't have it the way it was. Maybe it's the climax, if you think
like that, or maybe it's not. Maybe it's the thing that pushes to the
climax. It is not the epiphany, that old standby moment when the
sky opens and meaning shines down on the protagonist. The moment near the end, when the character stands at a window where
the raindrops are sliding down the pane; or looks at her lover and
sees how cruel he is; or loss suddenly fills his throat. (You get

some idea of how much I want you to think twice before jumping to epiphanies. See Charles Baxter's discussion of them in *Burning Down the House* for some reasons why.)

When students catch on to this idea and use it, they stop writing in circles, they start getting to the point, things happen, scenes matter, pulses build, and events and emotions escalate.

Stumble around awhile. Read and say, What came before? What happens after? What does this moment, this beat of action, do to the scene? To the line of beats? To the pulse? To the attitude of the protagonist? To the situation? How does it make the scene livelier or more menacing or funnier or more tender or brisker or sadder?

I'll point to focal points in some of the scenes to come. You look for them in your reading. And in your work. Next time you have a fuss, think about where it turned bad or didn't (I hope it didn't) and what happened next. Think about the time you went shopping and you realized you were too tired to keep at it. Or you saw yourself in a mirror trying on a sweater almost like one you already had and it made you mad at yourself that you'd spend money on something you didn't need. Maybe you carefully put things back. Maybe you dumped everything on a table. The rest of the scene fell away from that point, didn't it?

Your son or your daughter is telling you all the reasons why he or she needs to do something all the other kids are doing, and suddenly you realize he or she *has already done it*. What was the giveaway? The moment the kid said too much and didn't even know it? Or triggered a connection to something you remember that makes sense now? That synapse is your focal point. What you do next is the rest of the scene. (Now you know why I don't call all moments of recognition epiphanies: Focal points are workhorses, not stopping points, after which characters do things. They don't just stand and gape at the wonder of it all.)

Pam Houston's stories are full of these moments. I'm thinking of *Cowboys Are My Weakness*, wherein women either do things because they think they have to in order to win the big guys' hearts, or they finally get it that it's not worth it. Read some of her work. In a Lorrie Moore story, you may not see a focal point as it goes by, but you can go back and find it later. You work to read her stories, though you may not realize it at the time.

Some scenes seem to occur in the focal moment. Everything else is window dressing. In other scenes the focal moment is a window opening, a light flashing. Or there's something the protagonist was holding on to so tightly all along, and when we finally get to see it, we understand what's going on at last. Then the scene picks up motion.

See if it helps you to look for that instant, that image, that thought, that break, that turn, in your scenes. Pin it down, to be sure your scene has a point. An X.

PART TWO

THE HEART OF A SCENE

5
PULSE

HOW THE PULSE CARRIES ACTION AND EMOTION

THE PULSE OF A SCENE CARRIES ACTION AND EMOTION IN A STREAM OF CHARACTER NEED.

- HOW DO YOU KNOW WHAT THE PULSE OF YOUR SCENE IS?
- HOW DOES THE PULSE INTERACT WITH OTHER ELEMENTS OF THE SCENE?
- WHAT OBSCURES OR DILUTES THE IMPACT OF THE PULSE, WEAKENING THE SCENE?
- HOW DOES THE PULSE OF A SCENE RELATE TO THE NARRATIVE AS A WHOLE?
- EXERCISES

What is your scene's pulse?

First you ask yourself why you are writing this scene. What is its purpose in the narrative? That function must relate to the overall line of action in the story and help to pull the thread of reader concern through it. Then you ask:

> What element of this scene is its real heart? What matters most to the characters and will matter most to the reader?

Put it into words before you write or revise. For example:
• An immigrant bride wants some sense of control over her life in

the new country where she now lives. In a particular scene, it might be played out in how she handles the condescension of a butcher in the local store, or in her determination to learn how to drive.

• A recovered drug addict wants her children back from foster care. She is about to meet with her Children's Services caseworker to initiate her request.

• A detective is weary and pessimistic (and so he lets his guard down). The pulse can't just be negative, so what could his desire or need be? Maybe he wants to give one lousy bastard what he really deserves. Maybe he wants to stay alive until he retires in three months. Now imagine him in a scene with a mouthy lowlife in an unexpected confrontation.

• A child seeks comfort from the chaos of the household. What vulnerability could this set up in a scene? In other words, what might the child be willing to do, not knowing better?

• A retired woman's search for peace in a small town is upset when the new pastor shows up with a wife who was once the "other woman" who broke up her marriage to another man, not the pastor. What pulse is greater: her desire for serenity or the memory of her humiliation and pain? She meets the woman. Consider the difference in the direction of the scene, given the two pulses. (I got this straight out of an advice column.)

In each example, it is a *need* or *desire* that creates the pulse. Each scene has a dilemma or a pressure on the POV character, and it is sufficient in its importance that it drives the action and feeling. The pulse accelerates the scene; it is its engine, its combustion. The kind of story and its style will be intertwined with the nature and intensity of the pulse.

Hunger. Jealousy. Ambition. Lust. Maternal protectiveness. Sibling rivalry. These are examples of classic sources of pulses in stories. As I have suggested again and again: Start a list! Make it automatic to consider this in your rereading of stories you admire. (Don't stop to analyze stories the first time through. You'll lose the pleasure and the effect.)

How does the pulse interact with the other elements of the scene?

> The event must be sufficient to hold the actions that are fueled by the pulse.

In a scene, everything is woven together, as warp and weft in cloth. Actions must be clear and must rise in intensity. The reader has a sense that *something is happening* and, furthermore, that *something more is going to happen*. The scene must be well focused, and this is accomplished largely through a strong viewpoint. The meaning of the scene to its POV character establishes meaning for the reader. The reader understands what the actions mean to the character through the character's responses to the event.

What obscures or dilutes the impact of the pulse, weakening the scene?

Muddiness! Nothing so messes up a scene as disorganization, clutter, uncertainty, and failure to illuminate the need or desire of the POV character. The style of the writer and the demands of the narrative are going to influence the shape, length, and density of the scene. You may have long passages of interior musing, much necessary description, and blocks of dialogue; but if you do, it will be because in this scene, those words add to the awareness that something is happening and that it matters. It may also be because it is your style to reflect, digress, and extrapolate; if so, you must be controlled, focused, and very good with language!

Often, the apprentice writer overwrites a scene, plugging in much too much of all of the above, padding around undeveloped action. Or, worse yet, the writer fails to spell out much action at all, relying on the musing of the character to push the scene along.

> If you read a scene you have written and it is like walking through deep mud, start by identifying (a) the event, (b) the pulse, and (c) the beats; then, little by little, let the rest of it be added because it needs to be there.

How does the pulse of a scene relate to the narrative as a whole?

> There is a driving desire, need, or question that runs through a story.

It may not be obvious at the beginning, but awareness of the pulse should grow and become more urgent as the narrative progresses. Each scene should contribute to the intensity of that driving need or question. The pulse of the scene is like a current in a river, both pulled by and pushing the water. Of course there are times when the reader doesn't understand what the relationship is, but scenes should add up as the story progresses.

Examples
Raymond Carver's famous story "Cathedral" provides a marvelous example of this idea of the pulse in a scene. In this story, a woman has brought home an old friend, a man who is blind, and her husband is quite apprehensive about it. For one thing, he's never met a blind person. Late in the evening, they are "watching" TV and there is some talk about a cathedral. The blind man asks the protagonist to explain what a cathedral looks like, and when that turns out to be hard, the protagonist blurts out that he doesn't care about cathedrals, and the blind man says that's okay.

At that point, this story shifts radically. The blind man suggests that they draw a cathedral together. Now, all along, the scenes in this story have been underlaid with discomfort, but suddenly the two men, on the floor with a smoothed-out shopping bag and some ballpoints, are doing something important, and doing it together. Their shared sense of mission is the pulse. It's one of the most moving stories you'll ever read, and everything leads up to that closing scene.

Andre Dubus's story "The Fat Girl" is suspenseful even though you sense from the beginning that the protagonist is doomed. She grows up fat, but in college a close friend helps her slim down through torturous dieting. Her family marvels. She marries "a lean, tall, energetic man with the metabolism of a pencil sharpener" and gets pregnant. And then, oh then, "her desire for sweets was as vicious as it had been long ago."

One night her husband chides her. He says she'll want to get back into her bathing suit after the baby is born. She returns to her "world of secret gratification." She has a son, "brought him home, and nursed both him and her appetites." The tension between her and her husband grows and her girth expands. In the closing scene, they quarrel, then he pleads with her, but she is lost in the memory of her hunger, and then in the hunger itself. The pulse that has beat below the years has finally become a drum that drives her out of her marriage. It is her hunger! You should study this story to see how each and every sentence contributes to the overall effect of the story. The pulse is powerful—in the character, in each scene, and in the story. There is a brief scene where the girl flies home and her mother sees her thin for the first time and cries out, "You're beautiful!" That praise is the focal point of the scene; it becomes what sustains the girl for years.

The Swedish mystery writer Henning Mankell has written a series of books featuring a melancholy detective, Kurt Wallander. Interestingly, the main source of tension in Mankell's books lies not in the violent crimes, which, after all, take up only a few pages of the book, nor, to my mind, in the chases, which occur late in the long novels. Rather, the way that Mankell patiently spells out the enormous task of compiling evidence, sifting through it, creating hypotheses, and following up on them until something breaks—these are the elements of narrative that create tension. This relentless focus on solving the crime is the pulse of each and every scene, with the violent scenes pulled into a higher level of energy and expectation. It almost goes against logic to say it, but doggedness provides tension in his novels and, I think, is why certain readers like the "big thick" school of mysteries (Elizabeth George, P. D. James, Ian Rankin) more than the "fun reads" (like Sue Grafton): They enjoy slogging through every detail with the investigators and feeling they are in the thick of the setting.

As a reader of Mankell, I become aware of the enormous amount of work it takes to solve a crime, and I am privy to the way the work plays out. Wallander's brooding interiority slows down the action, and this actually increases the tension, because it keeps the reader from knowing the answers. I have to wait with Wallander. His obsessiveness is driven by his fearful awareness that a great global violence is impinging on this rural outpost of a cold, far-flung nation.

I had the pleasure of hearing Mankell speak, and he identified the pulse beneath his own motivation. He said that even in a remote Swedish landscape, people cannot escape violence. The knowledge that there is no safety anywhere is a powerful pulse to drive story—and to drive the writer himself.

Here is just a piece of a scene, from Mankell's *The Fifth Woman*, to give you an idea of how he does this:

> "Mapping out Eriksson's life is the first thing we have to do," Wallander said. "But before we start I want to try and give you my impression of the chronology of the crime."
> They were sitting at the big kitchen table. In the distance they

could see the crime-scene tape and the white plastic canopy flapping in the wind. Nyberg stood like a yellow-clad scarecrow in the mud. Wallander could imagine his weary, irritated voice. But he knew that Nyberg was talented and meticulous. If he waved his arms about he had a reason for it.

Wallander felt his attention begin to sharpen. He had done this many times before, and he could sense that at this moment the investigative team was starting to track the murder.

"I think it happened like this," Wallander began, speaking slowly. "Sometime after ten o'clock on Wednesday night, or maybe early Thursday morning, Holger Eriksson leaves his house. He doesn't lock the door because he intends to return soon. He takes a pair of night-vision binoculars with him. He walks down the path towards the ditch, over which he has laid a bridge. He's probably on his way to the tower. He's interested in birds. In September and October, the migratory birds head south . . . He steps onto the bridge, which breaks in two because the planks have been sawed almost all the way through. He falls into the ditch and is impaled on the stakes. That's where he dies . . ."

He poured some coffee from a thermos before he continued.

"That's how I think it happened," he said. "We end up with considerably more questions than answers. But it's where we have to start . . ."

Other members of the team add a few comments, and then they break up with their separate tasks. It's like watching someone build something when you aren't sure that they have a firm foundation. Will it get just so high and then fall over? Will it hurt someone? Note that the last paragraph is like a driver revving his engine. He says, ". . . we have to start." It takes the tension up a notch, just as a new threat would; the work of the investigation team is a counterbalance to the criminal's activity.

Such is the fascination of the police procedural. Everyone is focused on one thing: solving the crime. That is the pulse.

The best way I know to grasp the concept of pulse is to reread a story or a scene in a novel that has moved you, something that you remember and go back to. Then articulate for yourself what it is that is driving the scene and making it memorable. Do this again and again until it is second nature to your thinking and writing. Without a powerful pulse, your story won't be memorable to your reader, who won't tell her friend she ought to read it—you get the idea.

Anthony Doerr's exquisite story "The Hunter's Wife," from *The Shell Collector,* concerns the marriage of a hunter to a much younger woman. He lives in the wilderness and makes his living, in season, guiding hunters, so it is a shock when he discovers his future wife's uncanny ability to intuit animal perceptions. Ultimately, she is able to sense what the experience of the dead has become, and, from that, to offer comfort to the living. At the beginning of the story, the hunter takes the girl, who is only eighteen years old, to his cabin. It is winter. They go to see a hibernating bear. There's a built-in tension from the fact that disturbing a grizzly is pretty risky business. Besides that, of course, the hunter is falling in love with the girl, whose psyche is greatly affected by this wildness.

Watch for the escalation of the pulse in this scene:

> We can see him, he whispered, but we have to be dead quiet. Grizzlies are light hibernators. Sometimes all you do is step on twigs outside their dens and they're up.
>
> He began to dig at the snow. She stood back, her mouth open, eyes wide. Bent at the waist, he bailed snow back through his legs. He dug down three feet and then encountered a smooth icy crust covering a large hole in the base of the tree. Gently he dislodged plates of ice and lifted them aside. The opening was dark, as if he'd punched through to some dark cavern, some netherworld. From the hole the smell of bear came to her, like wet dog, like wild

mushrooms. The hunter removed some leaves. Beneath was a shaggy flank, a brown patch of fur.

He's on his back, the hunter whispered. This is his belly. His forelegs must be up here somewhere. He pointed to a place higher on the trunk.

She put one hand on his shoulder and knelt in the snow above the den. Her eyes were wide and unblinking. Her jaw hung open. Above her shoulder a star separated itself from the galaxy and melted through the sky. I want to touch him, she said. Her voice sounded loud and out of place in that wood, under the naked cedars.

Hush, he whispered. He shook his head no. You have to speak quietly.

Just for a minute.

No, he hissed. You're crazy. He tugged at her arm. She removed the mitten from her other hand with her teeth and reached down. He pulled at her again but lost his footing and fell back, clutching an empty mitten. As he watched, horrified, she turned and placed both hands, spread-fingered, in the thick shag of the bear's chest. Then she lowered her face, as if drinking from the snowy hollow, and pressed her lips to the bear's chest. Her entire head was inside the tree. She felt the soft, silver tips of its fur brush her cheeks. Against her nose one huge rib flexed slightly. She heard the lungs fill and then empty. She heard blood slug through veins.

Want to know what he dreams? she asked. Her voice echoed up through the tree and poured from the shorn ends of its hollowed branches. The hunter took his knife from his coat. Summer, her voice echoed. Blackberries. Trout. Dredging his flanks across river pebbles.

Now we turn again to Forster's Lucy Honeychurch, following her brief assignation with George in the violet-drenched countryside. She is back in the pensione. It is dark and rainy, and prudish Miss Bartlett is dead-set to turn the kiss into something horrible. Read this scene for the ferocity of its pulse; actually, for the clashing of the two women, the stuffy, hateful derision of Charlotte Bartlett, who will never have a man kiss her, against dear Lucy Honeychurch, who is in thrall to the passion that has risen in her in Italy—a passion for passion itself. It is Forster's great theme, the conflict of repressiveness and passion.

"So what is to be done?"

She was unprepared for the question. It had not occurred to her that she would have to do anything. A detailed exhibition of her emotions was all that she had counted upon.

"What is to be done? A point, dearest, which you alone can settle."

The rain was streaming down the black windows, and the great room felt damp and chilly. One candle burnt trembling on the chest of drawers close to Miss Bartlett's toque, which cast monstrous and fantastic shadows on the bolted door. A tram roared by in the dark, and Lucy felt unaccountably sad, though she had long since dried her eyes. She lifted them to the ceiling, where the griffins and bassoons were colourless and vague, the very ghosts of joy.

"It has been raining for nearly four hours," she said at last.

Miss Bartlett ignored the remark.

"How do you propose to silence him?"

"The driver?"

"My dear girl, no; Mr. George Emerson."

Lucy began to pace up and down the room.

"I don't understand," she said at last.

She understood very well, but she no longer wished to be absolutely truthful.

"How are you going to stop him talking about it?"

"I have a feeling that talk is a thing he will never do."

"I, too, intend to judge him charitably. But unfortunately I have met the type before. They seldom keep their exploits to themselves."

"Exploits?" cried Lucy, wincing under the horrible plural.

"My poor dear, did you suppose that this was his first? Come here and listen to me. I am only gathering it from his own remarks. Do you remember that day at lunch when he argued with Miss Alan that liking one person is an extra reason for liking another?"

"Yes," said Lucy, whom at the time the argument had pleased.

"Well, I am no prude. There is no need to call him a wicked young man, but obviously he is thoroughly unrefined. Let us put it down to his deplorable antecedents and education, if you wish. But we are no farther on with our question. What do you propose to do?"

An idea rushed across Lucy's brain, which, had she thought of it sooner and made it part of her, might have proved victorious.

"I propose to speak to him," said she.

Miss Bartlett uttered a cry of genuine alarm.

"You see, Charlotte, your kindness—I shall never forget it. But—as you said—it is my affair. Mine and his."

"And you are going to *implore* him, to *beg* him to keep silence?"

"Certainly not. There would be no difficulty. Whatever you ask him he answers, yes or no; then it is over. I have been frightened of him. But now I am not one little bit."

"But we fear him for you, dear. You are so young and inexperienced, you have lived among such nice people, that you cannot realize what men can be—how they can take a brutal pleasure in insulting a woman whom her sex does not protect and rally round. This afternoon, for example, if I had not arrived, what would have happened?"

"I can't think," said Lucy gravely.

Something in her voice made Miss Bartlett repeat her question, intoning it more vigorously.

"What would have happened if I hadn't arrived?"

"I can't think," said Lucy again.

"When he insulted you, how would you have replied?"

"I hadn't time to think. You came."

"Yes, but won't you tell me now what you would have done?"

"I should have—" She checked herself, and broke the sentence

off. She went up to the dripping window and strained her eyes
into the darkness. She would not think what she would have done.

What is sad, of course—for the time being—is that Lucy's
chaperone is able to dampen her ardent pulse. The next morning
they leave for Rome.

Exercises

• **Step Toward Desire:** Choose a character from your drafts who has
a strong desire line. Put him or her into a situation where it is possible to pursue something that might help reach a *step* toward the
thing desired. Create an obstacle and decide whether it is overcome.

• **"You Don't Get It!":** Put a character into a situation where she
feels misunderstood, and describe the ways that she either tries to
make herself heard, or else clams up and tries to get away unscathed.

• **Read for Desire Lines:** Read favorite scenes and write a sentence describing the need or desire of the POV character. See
how that desire line underlies the movement of the scene. Does
the scene further the character's progress toward the achieve-
ment, or impede it?

• **Escalating Desire:** Think of a scene in which a character is not
certain of the urgency of his desire, or what he will do about it.
Let the scene be about his realization that he must act. Don't let
the scene occur inside his head only, however; he comes to this
insight because of what happens in the scene. The faint pulse of
his desire grows stronger because of what he has to do. How does
the scene build that conviction? This is a scene of *escalation,*
driven by a character's response to exterior actions.

• **The Public Pulse:** Sit down with a daily newspaper and make
a list of the pulses that underlie the stories you read there; of

course you are free to imagine more than what the dry column told you! (Why do people sue each other? Testify before boards and committees? Commit crimes? Perform acts of heroism? Why do family members behave so badly with one another? And then refuse to press charges!)

• *Everybody's Got a Pulse:* Use characters from the Bible, from historical periods, or real members of your family and acquaintances to make statements about people that suggest pulses that might underlie stories about them. Think in terms of a story, and then try to pin down some imagined event, when the pulse "beats loudly" for your character. For example:

  a. Karla's mother has a distrust of outsiders; Karla announces her engagement to a man from a foreign country.

  b. For Peter, his family and home are the very embodiment of a successful life. Then he is served divorce papers from his wife.

  c. Charlotte is only eight, but she wants to be a ballerina. When a dance school opens in her little town, Charlotte brings home the flyer, but her mother says they can't afford lessons.

• *Look at Your Own Stories:* State the pulse in a sentence. Choose a scene and restate the pulse, making it specific to that part of the story. Now look at every aspect of the scene to see if it contributes to the pulse. How could you improve the scene by intensifying the pulse?

Now review the questions discussed in this chapter:

  • How do you know what the pulse of your scene is?
  • How does the pulse interact with the other elements of the scene?
  • What obscures or dilutes the impact of the pulse, weakening the scene?
  • How does the pulse of a scene relate to the narrative as a whole?

6

TENSION

HOW TENSION INCREASES READER INVOLVEMENT

OFTEN THERE IS A TAUT THREAD OF TENSION IN THE WEAVE OF A SCENE.

- WHAT IS MEANT BY "TENSION" IN A SCENE?
- HOW IS TENSION BUILT?
- HOW IS TENSION RELEASED?
- EXERCISES

What is meant by "tension" in a scene?

Tension is a source of intensity in a scene that provides focus and increases reader involvement.

Tension is the taut stretch of something pulled toward, away from, or through something, like the stretch of a rope in a game of tug-of-war. *It is caused when a question is raised and the reader's sense of anticipation is heightened.*

Tension advances the story by bringing an important question to the foreground. Will he kiss her? Will they get to the cellar before the tornado strikes? Will the drunken father strike his children? Will the wife learn of her husband's adultery? Will the soldier die from his wounds?

How is tension built?

You build tension by
- holding back information from the reader;
- introducing questions and then intensifying concerns about the answers;
- making the reader uneasy about the harmony of relationships.

Sometimes a scene builds tension and leaves the reader in a moment of caught suspense, not knowing what will happen. This sets up the reader for a later scene, a technique often used in books with multiple points of view, especially thrillers. (Some readers dislike this, finding it overly manipulative. Choose your technique based on what you like to read and who you think your readers will be.)

How is tension released?

Tension is released
- when adversaries move toward one another in a positive way to *resolve tension;*
- when adversaries step back from or defer the conflict; they *deflect or retreat;*
- when one of the adversaries *suppresses** the issue internally to avoid conflict;
- when one of the adversaries has a sudden *insight* that breaks the tension;
- when adversaries *escalate* the conflict into direct confrontation, possibly violence.

Keep in mind that tension can be released without direct confrontation, that is, by being dissipated. Someone can let go of the

---

* Tension is released only in the sense that it does not go further in the scene; it still exists, at least for the person who has suppressed it.

object or of the abstraction (emotion, concern, issue) being stretched. When tension is released in this way, the result may be one of mutual contentment, or it may simply be delaying conflict until later. It may be a yielding full of disappointment. How the tension is dissipated sets you up for later action in the story, or else closes this aspect of the story.

Another way for tension to be released is for the "thread" to break, evoking a moment of stark clarity and apprehension. This is a favorite way to create an epiphany—a sudden moment of insight (again, something you do not want to overuse).

Another general release is achieved through a kind of explosion, in which the conflict is played out until the tension breaks into climactic action or emotion. We expect this kind of tension breaker in high-action fiction; the challenge is to build intensity over the course of the book without wearing out the reader.

In all instances, you want to make the release of tension interesting and surprising; you don't want the outcome of the scene to be obvious from its beginning. We also see climactic tension breaks in literary fiction, but they tend to come from character rather than from pure plot and carry a deep sense of inexorability.

Examples

Robert Stone is a writer whose work is often taut with dread. His novel *A Flag for Sunrise* draws a group of mostly unseemly characters—and a nun—into the maelstrom of revolution in Central America. It is suspenseful from the beginning straight through to the end.

Likewise, his short story "Helping" is almost unbearably suspenseful, and you know it is going to be at the beginning, when Stone tells you that his protagonist, Elliot, is an alcoholic who has lately been sober. Then he says, "Sober, however, he remained, until the day a man named Blankenship came into the office at the state hospital for counseling." Although you now expect Blankenship to be the reason the narrator turns again to drink,

Stone is much more devious than that. The counseling session *sets in motion* Elliot's downfall. I've taken only a tiny slice of a moment in a story that is long and complex, with a powerful sense of inevitability even as it presents surprising turns.

Each of several scenes threatens to break into something awful but doesn't. Then Elliot goes home and his lawyer wife tells him about some bikers who got their case dismissed that day and threatened her. While they are talking about it, the bikers call, and Elliot, who has been drinking, ends up telling them that they should come on over. (His aggressiveness is a terrible blow to his fragile relationship with his wife.) He gets a gun and watches for them:

> ... From the window at which he sat, he commanded a view of several miles in the direction of East Ilford. The two-lane blacktop road that ran there was the only one along which an enemy could pass.
>
> He drank and watched the snow, toying with the safety of his 12-gauge Remington. He felt neither anxious nor angry now but only impatient to be done with whatever the night would bring. Drunkenness and the silent rhythm of the falling snow combined to make him feel outside of time and syntax.

This is only a small excerpt from a long passage of a long story, but reading it makes your heart race. Read the paragraphs again. Is there any doubt that something is going to happen? (It won't be what you think.)

Think of Andre Dubus III's *House of Sand and Fog,* in which both antagonists have claims on a house and neither will let go until tragedy ensues. One is the careless young woman who didn't bother to read her mail and so didn't discover a bureaucratic error that evicted her and put her house up for sale. The other is an Iranian immigrant slaving to give his family a proper home. He buys the forfeited home and then has to do battle with the woman, who is oddly passive yet frighteningly intrusive and stubborn. An entire family is literally destroyed.

In Paul Bowles's unforgettable story "A Distant Episode," a linguistics professor foolishly wanders away from town toward the Arabian Desert. He is unprepared for the snarling dogs, the gun pushed against his spine, the violence of his captors (all factors that escalate tension). By the time we see him again in the vicinity of the town, his tongue has been cut out and he has been trained like a dancing monkey. In the final scene, the horrible pressure of a year's captivity has built up until he "felt like roaring . . . So, bellowing as loud as he could, he attacked the house and its belongings." He attacks inanimate objects because he has been rendered powerless; the tension is dissipated by his impotence. A scary, brilliant story.

Some writers exploit tension and malice as a predominant strategy in their stories. I think of Margaret Atwood in her novels *Bodily Harm* and *Life Before Man,* and just about anything by the ferocious Mary Gaitskill, who slices through the terrible efforts of men and women to connect. Joy Williams is another writer whose work shivers with tension. Lynn Freed's fiction has a kind of scrim of dreamy menace, as if the world is off-kilter and her characters float just above danger. Diane Johnson's *Persian Nights,* set in Iran as it is on the cusp of the revolution against the Shah, is full of dread, as well as marvelous irony and the feel of a foreign culture.

In general, most fiction is tense without being scary or violent. Drama need not be bloody. Issues arise between people and sometimes divide them. I use the term *adversaries* to indicate that people are not in a state of agreement or consolidation, but it does not necessarily mean that there is open, physical conflict. For that matter, characters often do not even speak their minds openly, instead doing battle obliquely. Sometimes the tensest scenes of all are fought in *subtext,* which is made up of those things not said that bubble beneath the surface like so much boiling lava. When there is an underlying tension being suppressed while characters talk about something unrelated, it is said to be like having an elephant in the room. This can play out in innumerable ways. Anne Tyler is particularly adept at this kind of tension. Her characters are often too nice to quarrel, but that doesn't mean they don't have issues. The inability to talk about his grief over his son's murder breaks up Macon's marriage to Sarah in *The Accidental Tourist*.

In the most obvious case, two people share a problem but don't want to talk about it. In another situation, people talk about something, but one person is hiding facts or true feelings from the other. Either way, the underlying tension grows like yeast in a too-small jar, even if the exterior actions appear to have solved or deflected the conflict. People do not always say what they are feeling. When people don't speak honestly, misunderstandings grow into open anger or hardened resentment. (Ask any marriage counselor!) The seeds are planted for later conflict. Such divisions become mythic. Indeed, many of the conflicts in Eastern Europe and the Middle East go back centuries. Tribes, like families, carry the narratives of anger forward, generation to generation.

Think of how a character might behave after a quarrel in which she gave up, knowing she could not win, but after which she hoarded her bitterness. Her anger could burst forth later. Sublimation could make her act in small, insidious ways. Or perhaps she goes through a private struggle in which she is finally able to let go of the anger. How a character deals with hurt and bitterness tells a lot about him and also contributes to plot possibilities. If the character does one thing now, what will he do later?

In John L'Heureux's story "Departures," a mother feels rebuffed by her young son's rudeness when he comes home from the seminary on a visit. Rather full of himself, upon his arrival at the train station he chides her not to touch him. She is shocked and surely hurt, but she says nothing. Years later, on her deathbed, her feelings about the incident are made painfully clear to her son when the last thing she has to say is that she won't touch him, and that she "will be good." There is no opportunity for him to make things right.

How will your character handle anger, ridicule, or a sense of having been wounded? Imagining the answers to such questions can push you a long way toward conceiving a workable story. You simply start with a quarrel and imagine the aftermath. How should the responses be handled in your story? If the bitterness festers, how will it eventually erupt? If the wounded character is the consciousness of the story, you have to build passages of interiority, where the character works through emotions, weighs possibilities, and makes decisions.

Here is an example of tension dissipated by one character's apparent retreat from conflict. The brief scene sequence takes place during World War II, when Emma is a teenager and her mother, Greta, is a cook in Patty the Greek's café in Gallup, New Mexico. In this scene in the café, you will see that Emma appears to acquiesce to her mother's injunction, but as the story progresses it becomes clear that Emma does whatever she wants. You'll note also that she is on top of the original exchange, with the railroad man, until Greta interrupts. She is someone who expects to get her way.

One afternoon a railroad man sat down on the stool next to Emma. He was maybe five years older than her. He wore his trousers baggy and his shirt tight. "There's a movie with Claudette Colbert on," he said, "and I bet you just love her."

"I like her, but I don't love her. I love Bette Davis."

"We can see Bette Davis next time she's here," the railroad man said, and just then Greta seemed to be on top of them. A steak knife came down hard enough, it stuck on the counter, right in front of the railroad man's hand. He didn't flinch. He grinned.

"We're going home now, Emma," Greta said. "Get your coat." Emma didn't protest. <u>She got up with a little flick of her head.</u> The railroad man winked.

Patty yelled something as they went out the door, but with the tinkle of the bell on the door and the roar of a truck going by just then, Emma didn't hear what he said. Her mother was stiff with anger. She was mad a lot these days.

"He was just asking me out on a date," Emma ventured as they turned the corner and started toward their house on Terrace.

"If you were in school where you belong, you'd be meeting boys your own age," Greta said.

"Boys is right."

Greta stopped walking and looked Emma in the eye. "You will not date those railroad men," she said, and <u>Emma didn't even bother to argue.</u>

In both cases, Emma has to respond to her mother's instructions. Look at the underlined sentences. What is their effect on what appears to be acquiescence? What does it tell you about how Emma handles conflict?

The following scenes take place in Texas just after the beginning of World War II. A young woman, Grace, is on her way to be married to a man, Bucy, whom she does not love as much as she loves someone she can't have.

The passage is from Jane Roberts Wood's *Grace,* a novel of great delicacy, tenderness, and wisdom. In the first scene, Bucy proposes. In the second scene, Grace feels she must say something to him about her feelings for another man. Bucy demonstrates generosity and optimism.

Read the passage once for story, and then for how it displays the buildup of tension and its release. Notice how the dialogue is a negotiation between these two young people. Grace's attention to her passing surroundings is a way of evading the deep conflict she feels, until she finally must be honest, to her great relief.

Grace and Bucy had been at the Paramount Theater watching the movie *How Green Was My Valley* when the sound stopped, the screen went dark and the manager of the theater, looking like a Lilliputian after the giant, on-screen faces of Walter Pidgeon and Maureen O'Hara, came onstage and said, "President Roosevelt has just announced that Japan has attacked Pearl Harbor. We are now in a state of war with Japan."

Bucy had turned to her and said, "Where is Pearl Harbor?"

"I haven't any idea."

He took her hand and whispered into her ear, "Let's get married."

"Are you serious?"

"Dead serious."

Six days later they drove to Oklahoma to be married. By the time they reached Ardmore, snow had begun to fall, just a few flakes drifting down, but after Ardmore the wind rose, and the windows of Bucy's old Ford were not sealed. Afterwards she thought that only the intense cold made her turn and say, "Bucy, I have loved someone for quite a long time."

"Loved?"

"Love," she said firmly.

While she waited for him to speak, she saw a Burma Shave sign, read the first line. DOES YOUR HUSBAND MISBEHAVE? She smiled at Bucy, but he was looking straight ahead, his Adam's apple still for once. They drove past a pasture where three brown-and-white cows grazed. Just over the hill she saw the next line: GRUNT AND GRUMBLE? RANT AND RAVE? She had never heard Bucy rant or rave. And here was the last line, just ahead. She squinted her eyes to read: SHOOT THE BRUTE SOME BURMA SHAVE! Smiling at the word *brute,* she looked at Bucy.

"Bucy?" she said.

He reached for her hand and feeling how cold it was, he took gloves from the pocket of his overcoat and gave them to her.

"Just love me if you can," he said, and the grace of these words went to her heart. She moved close and drew his arm around her.

The first scene serves to set up the second. The turning point in their relationship occurs on the journey to be married. Because these are good and honest people, the tension lies in their silence. As soon as they speak, they solve the problem. You can clearly see the meaning for the characters of their subtle exchange, that is, the scene's *emotion*. Likewise, you can see that their shared knowledge of Grace's compromised heart, followed by her surprise at Bucy's acceptance of it, *shifts* their relationship to something more honest and loving, and makes their marriage possible. It is a lot for a "small" scene to accomplish so subtly.

Here is another scene where tension is released. In Lara Vapnyar's delightful story "Love Lessons—Mondays, 9 A.M.," an education student is tapped to teach a sex-education class to tenth-graders, and nearly perishes of self-consciousness. She has asked her aunt Galya for advice, but though she is teaching, she has grown to doubt it and fears discovery of her superstitious content: "What if lemon juice wasn't good enough as a contraceptive?" Besides that, she has a crush on another teacher. In this scene, she has gone to the school cafeteria for lunch.

I sat down at the teachers' table and began piercing my sardelki with a fork when Sergey tapped me on the shoulder. He stood grinning by my chair with a plate of herring and mashed potatoes. "Don't let them sneak away; make them work very hard!" He winked at me and walked to his usual place at the end of the table. My heart jumped up and down inside my chest. I spent the rest of the lunch break waiting for Sergey to continue. I chewed hard on the sardelki and shook the excess oil off the cubes of potato and beet. I was sure that Sergey had already thought of what to say; he was only waiting for the opportunity to speak. I had the terrifying thought that he somehow, through some unimaginable source, had become aware of Aunt Galya's existence and he would ask about her. I grew tired of waiting—I almost wished that Sergey would strike sooner. I stole a quick glance in his direction. He wasn't looking at me. He was working on his lunch, pulling bones out of the herring and laying them on the edge of his plate. It was a perfect chance to escape. I left my plate and hurried out of the cafeteria. I almost made it to the exit when I heard Sergey's voice again, rustling somewhere above my ears, the words barely audible amid the cafeteria's steady rumble. I had to lift up my face to make out what he was saying. He was asking me on a date.

You see that all the tension is built inside the narrator's worried mind.

- The *event:* The narrator eats lunch in an agony of self-consciousness in Sergey's presence.
- The *source of the tension:* Will he tease her about what she is teaching in her ill-prepared classes? Will she finally be humiliated the way she has expected to be since the first class she taught? (She's only a college student, called in because they are short-handed.)
- The *dissipation of the tension:* It is completely, unexpectedly, and happily broken when Sergey asks her on a date. Yet we had a kind of false turn before this, when she got up to leave, because, after anticipating that he would speak, she saw that he wasn't even looking at her.

In this short scene from William Brodrick's novel *The 6th Lamentation,* there is a wonderful mix of suspense and literary pleasure. A Gilbertine monk from England is trying to find another monk in Paris who may help him solve a mystery that goes all the way back to World War II. The overall tension comes from the need to find the man in order to know the truth. The immediate tension of this small scene is that the seeker doesn't know what to expect—the stranger has a reputation as being slightly mad—and the scene leaves us with the tension pulled taut.

Anselm made the final two-minute walk to the flat, climbed four floors of rough concrete stairs, and knocked firmly on the dull brown door. A small brass eyepiece stared back remorselessly.

The lights on the landing were broken, and thin streaks of grey daylight lay adrift upon the walls. Anselm heard a rattle from the other side, getting louder, as of air being pulled into thick lungs. An unseen cover scraped off the eyepiece. Anselm swallowed hard in the long, heaving interval that followed. The door opened slowly and smoothly.

In the gloom Anselm saw a shortish man, his wiry head pushed forward with a thick moustache falling over his mouth. All other features were indistinct, but Anselm was not really looking. His gaze had fixed upon the long knife.

Here, the author sets up an expectation of something risky by his description of the ascent of the stairs, and then cuts off the scene as Anselm sees the knife. Using another suspense strategy, the author then shifts to a scene about another character before coming back to Anselm.

- The *event*: Anselm arrives at the man's room.
- The *source of tension*: Will the man prove to be mad, as rumored?
- The *outcome*: We are left with the tension at a peak.

I think the *focal point* in this scene is the presentation of the knife; the scene breaks off arbitrarily; it is without an ending.

Similarly, mystery writer Cara Black writes a short scene in her novel *Murder in the Bastille* that leaves the reader hanging (but only for some white space, and then there's a follow-up scene):

Searing bursts of pain, a flashing staccato of agony and light hit Aimée. Then a heavy, hideous compression jammed her skull. Spread across her cranium, leveled her. Like nothing she'd ever felt.

She opened her mouth with a cry that took all the air from her. Her universe, cliffs and peaks of hurt, throbbed. A shimmery cold spiked her spine. Everything folded into dark; all was furry and fuzzy.

And then she threw up. Everywhere. All down her Chinese silk jacket. She reached out to what felt like leaves, wet with clingy bits of vomit. Then she fell over, her nails scraping the stone. Night starlings tittered above her.

René's voice sounded faraway. "Aimée! Aimée! What happened? Are you hurt? Are you still there?"

René was still on the phone . . . but he was so far away. She tried to speak but her mouth wouldn't work. No words came out. No rescue plea. No sound.

- The *event:* A woman talking on the phone is suddenly stricken with a horrible illness.
- The *source of tension:* What's wrong? What's happening? Will she survive?
- As in the scene with the monk, we are left with the tension still in place. That worry carries us into the next scene.

In Monica Wood's fine book of linked stories, *Ernie's Ark,* a town is in crisis because of a paper-mill strike. In one long scene, the CEO, Henry John McCoy, drives with his daughter to see the site, and their presence incurs the wrath of the strikers. There is a double layer of tension in this scene, because the father and daughter disagree about the strike, as well as about how the daughter is living her life. Here is an excerpt.

"They're tired," my daughter tells me. "They're hard-bitten and lost. What they want is so ordinary. Don't you see that, Daddy?"

"The one on the end. Blue-and-red jacket."

"What about him?" She's suspicious now.

"He bought your braces."

She sits back in the driver's seat and folds her arms, staring ahead.

"The one right next to him paid for your voice lessons. His son footed the bill for Harvard."

"Don't make me your accomplice, Daddy."

"If you want to interrogate some assumptions, my girl, you can start with your own innocence. Why don't you boycott paper until this is over, put off your dissertation for a few months?" . . .

All at once the gate lights come on, activated by the darkening mist. The picket line stirs lightly, a hint of motion that appears to me rife with menace. A sound comes from their midst, a shout of uncertainty mixed with outrage, then the sound takes the shape of a question and the small, edgy pack shifts toward us with the precision of birds changing direction and my daughter is making a sound like a surprised squirrel.

"Start the car, Emily," I say. I try messing with the buttons to get out of the cradle of this seat and can't find the right ones, end up in a perfect position to be stabbed in the belly if someone so desired. "Emily. Start the car."

They are upon us now, a ring of faces peering at us from the murk, about six of them, backlighted by the safety lights around the gate, their faces feverish and easy to interpret. I start jabbing buttons at random, trying to get myself worked into a more manly pose. My window sinks soundlessly down.

I hear my name, hear some expletives and two or three obscenities entirely new to me and regional in a way I didn't expect. I admit my identity. I tell them just who I am. Out of nowhere, like a magician's trick, they produce a couple of baseball bats, fine blond small bats of the sort you might see on a Little League field.

"Oh my God Daddy oh my God Daddy," my daughter is calling, and the sound of the revving motor fuses with the first downward chop of a bat on the hood and my daughter's high-pitched squeal. The fog lifts and lowers, lifts and lowers, and I see them in pieces—a frayed shirttail, a tuft of hair, a twisted lip. I see a raised arm, the rounded tip of a bat, then hear the splintering of one six-hundred-dollar headlight. For a few moments there is nothing but sound, an enraged battering, high cries inside the car and low grunts and murmurs outside, the nails-on-chalkboard grind of the engine, which my daughter is trying to turn over and over, not realizing it's already on. She is banging on the console, engaging the wipers, the locks, the air-conditioning, as the windows rise and fall. Finally there is silence. The men stop. My shrieking daughter turns the wheel and the men stand back with no more passion than if we were a taxi pulling away from the curb.

Wood makes you feel you are in the car with the narrator and his daughter, in flight from a mob. The turn in the scene occurs when the lights come on; that paragraph, the focal point, is the boiling up of the men into a dangerous threat that explodes. Then the tension is broken at its highest point, and released. The building up of details and the curtness of the prose make you anxious, until the silence. "The men stop." They drive away.

One of the reasons the stories in this book are so pleasurable—and so instructive—is that the sources of conflict vary widely and are keenly drawn in the depiction of characters living ordinary lives.

Sex in fiction, by the way, needs tension, too. It's often a question of who has the power, the say (how much? how soon?), whether seduction is subtle or overt, or whether it is seduction at all. In life, sex is about two people wanting the same thing at the same time. In fiction, a placid scene is boring, although a sex scene can be ruminative, tender, etc. Tension doesn't have to be negative; it can be playful, or simply the result of a desire to please when there is an outside worry in the bedroom.

Dan Chaon nicely illustrates "wires crossed" between a husband and wife in "I Demand to Know Where You're Taking Me," a wildly funny, offbeat story about Cheryl, who lives among her husband's oddball clan and is starting to feel very creepy about one of his brothers, who is in prison. The husband is a lawyer trying to get his brother out; the wife is starting to believe the brother is guilty. Worse, the brother keeps calling her. *And* she's babysitting the brother's foul-mouthed parrot!

There are two scenes, like bookmarks, that show the effect of the couple's unresolved tension on their affections—and their sex lives. Here's the first scene.

She waited up. But when he finally came into the bedroom he seemed annoyed that she was still awake, and he took off his clothes silently, turning off the light before he slipped into bed, a distance emanating from him. She pressed her breasts against his back, her arms wrapped around him, but he was still. She rubbed her feet against his, and he let out a slow, disinterested breath.

"What are you thinking about," she said, and he shifted his legs.

"I don't know," he said. "Thinking about Wendell again, I suppose."

"It will be all right," she said, though she felt the weight of her own dishonesty settle over her. "I know it." She smoothed her hand across his hair.

"You're not a lawyer," he said. "You don't know how badly flawed the legal system is."

"Well," she said.

"It's a joke," he said. "I mean, the prosecutor didn't prove his case. All he did was parade a bunch of victims across the stage. How can you compete with that? It's all drama."

"Yes," she said. She kissed the back of his neck, but he was already drifting into sleep, or pretending to. He shrugged against her arms, nuzzling into his pillow.

The second scene occurs on an evening when one of the kids has repeated something the bird said. In this scene, the husband, Tobe, has apologized, but Cheryl is feeling unsettled. She is sitting on the bed reading, and Tobe sits down beside her.

She closed her eyes as Tobe put the back of his fingers to her earlobe, stroking.

"Poor baby," he said. "What's wrong? You seem really depressed lately."

After a moment, she shrugged. "I don't know," she said. "I guess I am."

"I'm sorry," he said. "I know I've been really distracted, with Wendell and everything." She watched as he sipped thoughtfully from the glass of beer he'd brought with him. Soon, he would disappear into his office, with the papers he had to prepare for tomorrow.

"It's not you," she said, after a moment. "Maybe it's the weather," she said.

"Yeah," Tobe said. He gave her a puzzled look. For he knew that there was a time when she would have told him, she would have plunged ahead, carefully but deliberately, until she had made her points. That was what he had expected.

But now she didn't elaborate. Something—she couldn't say what—made her withdraw, and instead she smiled for him. "It's okay," she said.

You certainly wouldn't describe this as a sexy scene. But why not? They're married, they're in the bedroom, he touches her. There's too much tension between them, that's why; and too much on her mind—withheld from her husband—for her to be able to respond to her husband's small gesture with any affection. The best she can do is try to reassure him, an uneasy tamping down of tension. This is "suppression."

There is a tender moment at the end of *A Room with a View* when Lucy and George, now married, are back in the Florence pensione where they met. There is the gentle pretense of tension, all the sweeter to break for a kiss.

George said it was his old room.

"No, it isn't," said Lucy; "because it is the room I had, and I had your father's room. I forget why; Charlotte made me, for some reason."

He knelt on the tiled floor, and laid his face in her lap.

"George, you baby, get up."

"Why shouldn't I be a baby?" murmured George.

Unable to answer this question, she put down his sock, which she was trying to mend, and gazed out through the window. It was evening and again the spring.

"Oh, bother Charlotte," she said thoughtfully. "What can such people be made of?"

"Same stuff as parsons are made of."

"Nonsense!"

"Quite right. It is nonsense."

"Now you get up off the cold floor, or you'll be starting rheumatism next, and you stop laughing and being so silly."

"Why shouldn't I laugh?" he asked, pinning her with his elbows, and advancing his face to hers. "What's there to cry at? Kiss me here." He indicated the spot where a kiss would be welcome.

Arrivals

There is something else I want you to think about, and that is the balance of inevitability and surprise, the pleasure we get when we arrive at insight at the same time a character does. A character makes a choice we did not expect, and instantly we see that there was no other choice to be made. Watch for such moments in stories; they are rarer than you might think. When you come to such a moment, mark that story or passage and come back to study how it was structured.

Surprise that comes out of gratuitous coincidence or shock isn't good storytelling. Real surprise, the alleviation of true tension, is earned.

Exercises

Read many scenes and identify the source of the tension and what happens to it. See what makes it intensify; see what makes it dissipate or erupt. If you make simple notes, you can come back to them and use them as story starters for practice, putting your own spin on the initial ideas.

To make a note of a good scene in which the pulse is one of growing tension, think of the scene as a series of movements toward the release.

Write a sentence that summarizes the tension, and another that summarizes the release.

Write a list of the steps that build the tension.

Plan a scene by thinking of an event that will "contain" what you want to happen. Then you can follow the same approach as in describing another author's scene; write a two-part summary. If you decide a scene appeals to you strongly, of course go ahead and write it fully.

- *Intersection:* Here are two "ways in" to a tense scene.
  a. Think of a "terrible moment," a predicament that a character is in. Now, thinking in a backward jump, imagine what precipitates the problem: What situation does the character find himself in, and how does he get there? How does he handle it? *It will make a lot of difference whether the character is expecting the problem or if it is a surprise.*
  b. Plan a scene that starts with no apparent problem. Set your character in an ordinary activity and then introduce the first hint of a threat, then another, until something occurs to put the character in danger. Don't let him recognize the danger right away. You can leave him there, and leave the rescue to a follow-up scene. *You have to think of this scene as an intersection of the expected with the unexpected.* This could be as simple as people on a stroll who stumble into trouble.

- *The Elephant in the Room:* Put two or more people in a situation where they have something to do and that's all they talk about, as a way to avoid the real issue they are avoiding. For example, family members cleaning out the bedroom of a loved one after a funeral; a wife visiting her husband in prison; lovers who both know that one has been unfaithful. The possibilities are infinite.

• *Conflict Redux:* Write a summary of a deep family conflict that erupted a year ago. Now imagine a scene in which the family is gathered again (for what occasion?). How will they handle the old subject? Will it resurface? Choose a POV character carefully. You may want to write two scenes, one from the past, one in the present. Remember to have a reason for the family to gather; give the family something to do *into which the conflict surfaces.*

• *Self-evaluation:* Look at scenes you have written that utilize tension. Reduce them to two summary statements, one that explains the *tension,* and the other that explains the *release.* Note what shifts or changes with the release. Choose a scene to rewrite. Try to *heighten the tension* by making your writing tighter and more focused. *Sharpen the release.* Alternatively, see what happens if you try to draw the tension out, maintaining its energy and the question of what will be the outcome.

Now answer the questions discussed in the chapter:
- What is meant by *tension* in a scene?
- How is tension built?
- How is tension released?

7

NEGOTIATION

AN ALTERNATIVE VIEW OF CONFLICT

THERE ARE WAYS TO THINK OF CONFLICT AS SOMETHING
OTHER THAN DIRECT CONFRONTATION.

- FICTION AS A PROCESS OF CHANGE
- NEGOTIATION AS A MEANS OF RESOLVING CONFLICT
- EXERCISES

Fiction as a process of change

Everyone says that conflict is at the heart of story. Well, almost everyone. Author and teacher Carol Bly says that the word *conflict* is part of the language of war, and she resists the vocabulary it suggests, like "hitting the mark" or "attacking the subject." She also points out—usefully, I believe—that it is too easy to think of conflict as two people butting heads, instead of recognizing the complications and subtleties of story, in which many issues are at play.

I realized some time ago that I don't think about conflict in every story, either, though I'm always asking myself, What's in play here? Writer and teacher Oakley Hall says of fiction that it is "a process of change, and the heart of interior change is discovery or recognition, the revelation of something not comprehended before." (This is a good definition of epiphany, but Hall grounds discovery in solid action.) He also discusses promises kept and broken. Of course there are all kinds of ways that conflict can arise in situations constructed around these concepts, but thinking in terms of secrets and promises seems very contemporary, perhaps because we are so imbued with psychological precepts. In the end, it comes back to the need for the presence of *tension* in a story.

There are certain kinds of stories that are likely to have direct confrontations—think of Westerns, thrillers, most mysteries*— but in most instances, the number of passages in a story in which outright anger is expressed is likely to be very small. Rather, we see characters dancing around issues, slicing at topics that don't really have much to do with the real source of tension. Or we see arguments cut short, delayed for a later time. And in many instances, what we see is *negotiation,* an exchange of character desires and denials and relenting, until some sort of peace is carved out, or else the whole interaction falls apart.

Examples

I love Diane Glancy's short novel *Flutie* for its lovely heart and piercing knowledge. Set in a gritty plains landscape, it tells about the passage to adulthood of a deeply religious teenage girl who feels she is "without a tongue," and so does not speak outside the home. I've chosen two passages that may on first glance seem to demonstrate conflict, but I think of them as failed negotiations, instances in which the balance of power is so uneven that the weaker person is unable to gain any foothold toward what he or she desires.

The first passage is about Flutie's older brother. I'll discuss the combination of summary and scene later. I've marked the scenes with superscript numerals.

> Franklin wanted to quit school and his father wouldn't let him. He was nineteen years old, nearly twenty, and he wasn't

---

* The exception, most of the way through them, is in the category called "cozy mysteries," where the violence is offstage and there's lots of local color and character.

going back. They argued about it in the mornings when Flutie's mother slammed the skillet on the stove. Flutie was already fifteen. She was going to pass him in school.*

Franklin's friends had quit, he argued. He wasn't going to be the oldest in school. He held his head with a hangover.

[1]"A lot of them kids are older," his mother said. "They got to help with the haying. They can't always hide in the library reading them books." Flutie's mother looked at her.

Franklin's father wouldn't let up. If Franklin finished high school, he could go to college and learn accounting. They could buy the garage and run it. They wouldn't always be at a loss.

Franklin tried to eat his eggs† with his father yelling in his face. He would leave Vini, he said. He would go to Fort Sill in Lawton and join the army.

"How'd you make it in the army? You can't even get out of bed in the morning." Franklin's father threw his toast at Franklin. Franklin flung his plate at his father.

"Get out of here, Franklin," Flutie's mother said, "you're going too far."

Franklin bolted from the kitchen and roared down the road in his truck as Flutie's mother wrestled with her husband to hold him in the kitchen.

[2]Later that evening, when Flutie returned from Ruther and Luther's, Flutie's father put the tarp over the sweat-lodge frame in the backyard. He built a fire in the pit and heated the rocks.

[3]When Franklin came back drunk, Flutie's father dragged Franklin into the sweat lodge. Flutie listened to Franklin yell as his father pounded him. She heard him plead to get out of the sweat lodge that was hotter than his father's anger, hotter than their feeling of hopelessness, hotter than the failure that hedged them on the western Oklahoma plains.

She heard Franklin get sick. She heard her father cry.

---

* Paragraph of narrative summary: a statement of "the way things were" with Franklin and his family.

† A transition into the specific time: morning, breakfast, when the argument is out in the open.

Her mother sat in the kitchen holding a wet rag over her dark eye.

When the mother's dialogue begins, the real scene begins (1), and continues until Franklin bolts, and his mother has to hold back the father. Note that much of the dialogue is given as *indirect discourse,* meaning that it is summarized rather than rendered; then, at other places, the actual dialogue is presented. This makes the scene economical.

The second scene (2) is "Later that evening," and although it is summarized, we do know the beats of the scene that took place: Flutie comes home to see her father put the tarp over the frame and then build a fire.

The third scene (3) begins when Franklin returns. It is presented obliquely, through Flutie's apprehension of what is going on as she hears them fighting, and the aftermath of the fight. In the last sentence, Glancy pulls the reader to the mother, powerless in the kitchen chair.

Much later in the book, Flutie has a job pumping gas, and a friend, Jess, who helps her escape the household, where things are no better despite Franklin's absence. But when Jess says he wants to marry her, she goes over it in her mind, weighing what she would have—a house up the road (but it is his family's house), a place where she could visit with Franklin's wife, maybe flowers— and the something that "lodged in her throat" at the thought.

She is nineteen, though, and her parents want her settled. These two short scenes are about her refusal to marry Jess.

"I don't want to marry Jess."

"Get your belongings from the attic room," Flutie's mother told her. "He's coming for you."

"What's wrong?" her father asked.

"I just don't want to live with them."

Flutie's mother laughed. "It's too late. The minister's waiting at the church."

"Franklin and Swallow live in the trailer park now. You got room," Flutie said.

Flutie's mother threw a cardboard box at her.

"It'll feel like I'm all tied up," Flutie said.

She carried the box upstairs and threw her picture of Jesus into it. Her box of rocks and salt crystals and scraps of deer-hide and the prehistoric fish bone. But she smashed the papier-mâché volcano against the wall.

"I can't marry you, Jess," Flutie handed him the box as she came down the stairs. "I can't."

He opened the backdoor for her.

"Just leave without me," Flutie said.

"Get in the truck," Jess told her.

"No," Flutie answered, and walked through the yard toward the field.

He came after her, pulled her arm. She jerked away from him and ran.

She heard Jess calling after her.

"You ain't comin' back," her mother yelled. "You just live with the deer."

Flutie heard Jess tear down the road in a flush of gravel as she crossed the field.

She would keep walking and wouldn't stop until she reached Ruther's.

These two affecting scenes make up a major turning point in the novel, so they are rendered in detail, though they are short. Flutie has no apparent power, and there seems to be nothing for her to take into a negotiation, but she seizes power over her own fate.

In her wonderful story "Saint Chola," K. Kvashay-Boyle writes a scene of confrontation between a junior high school girl and an adult who is in for a surprise. The event is a minor accident in the street, but the action of the scene is the aftermath. Note how it is a series of reactions, one character to the other, until the narrator seizes control. Some would say that the narrator and the man who is trying to bully her are in conflict, but I think you can also describe them as being engaged in a *negotiation:* Who is going to decide how the incident is treated? Happily, it's the girl; note how this is accomplished as she builds authority by her insistence that since she is the injured party, she will decide what is to happen, and by drawing on the resources she feels as a junior high school girl. Notice, too, how she ignores the suggestion by one of her friends that they leave the scene, a suggestion that feeds the man's argument, but does not impress the narrator or lessen her resolve. Furthermore, she changes the terms of the negotiation: It's no longer about whether she will leave, but about whether she will have a record of the incident.

On the way home from school you get knocked down by a car. With a group of kids. It's not that bad, kind of just a scary bump, from the guy doing a California-stop, which means rolling through the stop sign. At first he says sorry and you say it's okay. But when you suck up all your might and ask to write down his license plate number he says no. Your dad must be a lawyer, he says, is that it? What, look, you're not even hurt, okay? Just go home.

You have some friends with you. You guys were talking how you could totally be models for a United Benetton ad if someone just took a picture of you guys right now. You're on your way to Tommy's Snack Shack for curly fries and an Orange Julius. Uhh, I think we should probably just go, all right? Noel says. It's not that bad so we should just go.

Yeah, go, the man says. Don't be a brat, he says. Just go.

Okay fine, you say, fine, I'll go, but FIRST I'm gonna write it down.

He's tall and he looks toward the ground to look at you. Just mind your own business, kid, she doesn't want you to. No one wants you to, he says.

Well I'm gonna, you say.

Look, you're not hurt, nobody's hurt, what do you need to for?

Just in case, you say. If it scares him you're happy. You're in junior high. You know what to do. Stand your ground. Make your face impassive. You are made of stone. You repeat it more slowly just to see if it freaks him out. *Just. In. Case,* you say and you're twelve and if you're a brat then wear it like a badge.

This is a passage about empowerment, pure and simple.

Think of a time you had to negotiate your rights with someone who wanted authority over you. Step away from memories of your parents or your teachers, as they are too obvious. And of course you can invent an incident.

I remember once I got out of the car to argue about a parking space in our pleasant little town, and a guy got out of his pickup carrying a shotgun! I had my three-year-old daughter with me, and right then I decided I would never again care about my "rights" to such stupid things; it was a big step in becoming a real adult, something the jerk with the gun obviously was not.

Now let's look at a scene built almost entirely of dialogue, in which the negotiation seems to be about whether a man, Abel, will be able to rent a house from its owner, Eloise. The scene makes quite a turn, a little bit comic, a little sly, and very satisfying. (Both characters are elderly.) It is from Annette Sanford's story "Housekeeping." Note the points when the subject of the dialogue shifts; note, also, the point at which Abel touches Eloise.

Eloise fixed a picnic and took it out when the hammering stopped. She meant for them to eat on the cottage lawn, but they ate in the thicket because an early thrush mixed-up on the seasons was singing its heart out and she wanted to hear.

They sat on her bench and spread out the food on a folding table.

"This is good," Abel said about baked beans and wieners.

"Try some of this." Mustard chow-chow she had made herself.

With the meal under way, she made an announcement. "I have halfway decided you can live in my house."

"Halfway?" he said.

"I have to know first if you're a con man."

He whooped at that. "Do you think if I was I'd tell you yes?"

"Are you or aren't you? Tell me straight."

"I am not a con man."

"You understand, don't you, what I mean by that?"

"I think I do. A liar and a cheat who might slicker you out of whatever you own."

"That's it exactly." She folded her hands. "And you say you aren't? Can I believe you?"

"It's the truth, Eloise. Would you pass the grapes?"

She ate the banana she had previously intended to slice over cereal and eat in the kitchen. "Grace says it all fits together for you to be crooked."

"Grace." He frowned. "Grace from across the street? Who ducks into the garage when she thinks I've seen her?"

"She thinks your walk gives you away, that you were smooth as a tick's back, the way you worked me."

He nodded agreeably. "I did some of that."

"Mowing the lawns? Bringing me supper?"

"And playing the violin. I thought you'd enjoy it."

"You didn't play well."

"I played well enough to put you to sleep." He ate a cracker. "I worked you another time, to get the preserves."

"Grace thinks you want to get my house."

"I want to live in it awhile and see how it feels to get out of that trailer."

"What if you like it?"

"Maybe I'll buy it."

"Do you have any money?"

"Enough," he said.

The bird sang again from a farther place, whistling purer than air or water.

Eloise said: "What have you been doing for most of your life?"

"Smoking for one thing. But I gave it up." He leaned back and thought. "I drilled oil wells. I built a few houses. Mostly," he said, "I've gone around looking." He gave her a grin. "For more lawns to mow. What about you?"

"I've been right here. Teaching," she said. "And picking figs."

"Why didn't you marry?"

"Why should I marry? I was in love with teaching. And I had my parents."

She picked a leaf and folded it neatly. "Have you given any thought to the shape of the year?"

"The year?" He chuckled. "I can't say I have."

"Have you ever noticed that it's winter on one end and on the other end too?"

He took her hand, a child's hand in the palm of his, and squeezed it lightly. "If you were in charge, how would you arrange it?"

"I'd start with summer and end with spring." She let his thumb trace the moons of her fingernails, though her mouth was dry and her heart was knocking. "Grace says—"

He gave a mild groan.

"She says I ought to know you longer before I trust you."

"You can tell Grace people our age can't waste time on long engagements."

"Engagements!" she said.

"Just a manner of speaking, Eloise."

"We are not engaged."

"We are not," he agreed.

She let her heart calm down before she spoke again. "Have you ever been married?"

"Once," he said. "For about thirty minutes."

"Why didn't it last?"

"We didn't like each other."

"Abel," she said, "you may live in my cottage if you tell me truthfully you have no interest in making a match."

"A match." He smiled. "You mean like a couple? Miss El," he said, "I will never legally or criminally seize your house."

"It's not the house alone." She went ahead fearfully. "It's what you might think because I'm letting you live in it."

"I might think you care for me."

"Yes," she said. "I wouldn't want to mislead you."

He chuckled again. "You *don't* care for me."

"I don't care for marriage."

"Would you care to explain?"

"I'm not sure I can."

"Try, why don't you?"

She started slowly and gathered steam. "I've lived by myself for too many years. I have to have my own room. I like to read late. I get up and take medicine. And I'm used to playing the radio all night if I want."

He waited quietly.

"And sex," she burst out with a bravery unknown to her. "The very idea of it gives me a stomachache."

"Scares you," he said.

"Scares me to death."

They listened to the bird in the thicket again. When it flew, Abel said, "I've lived by myself most of my life. I need my own room. I watch TV until two in the morning. I get up and take walks. And sex at my age is not to be counted on."

"Well," said Eloise, "I'm glad that's settled."

"It's good," he agreed, "to have it out of the way."

They sat awhile longer. When the fireflies came out she began putting things in the picnic hamper.

"Would you like more tea?"

"Tea? No, thank you." He stopped her hands from folding the tablecloth. "Tell me again about your year."

"I'd start it in June."

"So that would mean that right about now it's the middle of January?"

"Yes." She laughed. "Can't you tell it's cooler?"

"By July, your time, I'll be through with the house. Is that long enough to get over a scare?"

"Six months? Oh, no. No, I don't think so."

"How long will it take?"

He felt her tremble. "Maybe till Christmas."

"Dear girl," he soothed. "July *is* Christmas."

"I mean next year."

"Miss El," he whispered. He put an arm around her. "I would never rush you but by any calendar it's time we kissed."

"Oh, Abel, we can't! It's not dark yet."

"Close your eyes, sweet heart, and you'll see that it is."

Isn't the craft in this scene something to admire? Notice how the power shifts back and forth, until both parties have what they want, and neither has had to give up anything. I wouldn't call that conflict. The author controls the rhythm of the scene by interspersing the dialogue with beats of action that also escalate the sexual tension and keep us oriented as to where they are, physically, in the scene. The whole thing reads as if it just glided off the writer's fingers, but I'm sure you'll agree that it represents real skill and care and a whole lot of heart.

In a complete change of tone, let's look at a story by Victoria Lancelotta. This one is called "Nice Girl." The girl's sister was drowned when they were eight and five, the surviving girl the younger; it has destroyed her ability to mature, trust, and love. The following scene, we are given to understand, is one that occurs often. The mother reaches out to her daughter, but the girl refuses her overture, and the negotiation, in truth, is never even conducted. It is a sad, oblique moment that occurs after the prior scene, a visit to the dead child's grave. I have indicated the scenes with superscript numerals.

[1]Thirteen on a Sunday with my parents after Mass—stuffed animals in baskets, prayer cards, a box of sugar candy for Valen-

tine's Day—*kiss me, be mine*. My father propped these things against the headstone, the offering of the living, while my mother gripped my thin arm and did not cry. Tears were a luxury, a temptation, like meat on Fridays: the first step on the path to a place she would not go.

Once home, we separated, my father in the living room and me in the bedroom with my schoolbooks while my mother wandered the house, silent in stocking feet. This lasted until she could wait no longer and came to stand outside my closed door, still for some minutes before knocking.

[2]"Will you come for a walk with me?" she said, waiting, still, watching for a sign from me that this was where we'd start, our words like sucking whirlpools to finish us off on a sunny winter afternoon.

Watchful me, fingerprints inked on pages—"I can't now," the *now* my constant mistake, the thing that gave her license to come back the next Sunday, and the next, to ask me to walk with her I thought until the day I died.

"You shouldn't work so much," she said. "Why do you work so much?"

I am afraid, also, of dying. I was afraid of that early, a quick and restless fear. I imagined I would die in a car wreck, strapped in and burnt or else tossed from an open window or thrown through glass, eaten by gravel or hard earth—I would not die in water, not that.

There is a brief first scene (1) at the cemetery, with a last line of commentary about her mother's fear of crying. Then there is a paragraph of transition (here, a narrative summary) that orients us to their home base and how they arrange themselves there, until the mother approaches the girl's door. The second scene (2) begins when her mother asks her to walk with her; the girl claims to have too much schoolwork, and the mother, rebuffed, switches the subject to the daughter's work: "Why do you work so much?" She has no way to press for what she really wants, no power to negotiate.

The last paragraph is a reflection; the narrator speaks of her fear of dying. Everything in the story has to do with that; certainly the two prior scenes do. Fear and sorrow are the underlying pulse of the scene. How can anything be "negotiated" when the real issue is never discussed, perhaps can never be discussed?

Exercises

• **Compiling Strategies:** Compile a list of strategies that characters use to argue or connive to get their way with other characters; take these from scenes within stories you admire. (Better yet: Take them from life.) Write brief scene or story summaries that employ these strategies, making them your own. Don't worry about writing whole stories. Just work through scenes that incorporate types of character behavior you have not tried before. This expands your sense of possibilities in your own writing.

• **Suppressed Defiance:** Write a scene in which one character is more or less powerless and is being ordered to do something by a person in authority. Let the respect and/or love of the underdog character keep him from openly defying the order, but find a way to express the tension building inside. You can do this through physical movements, interior responses, attempts to reason with the person, or other strategies of your invention. Work toward closure that either shifts the position of power or reaffirms it.

• **Open Defiance:** Write a scene in which there is an imbalance of power between characters, but the weaker person will not accept it. How is the resistance expressed? Does it result in a change in the balance? In the relationship? Are things worsened? Remember, you can have more than two people in a scene!

• **Pull-away Love:** Write a scene between lovers in which one has begun to pull away from the relationship and the other is struggling to keep things as they were. You will need to have a subject for the scene, something for them to be negotiating, such as participation in an upcoming event. This can also be thought of as an *avoidance* scene. One lover is avoiding dealing with the problem; the other is avoiding having to face it at all. This is a good example of a setup for a scene with strong subtext.

Watch for scenes where the desires of characters are going in different directions (are in conflict?) and see how they try to get what they want. Once in a while a character will yell at the top of her lungs or put up his fists, but most of the time you will see attempts at manipulation, negotiation, subterfuge, flattery, or any other strategy that works for victory without drawing blood. Every writer approaches this differently, in different stories.

8

IMAGES

WRITING THAT APPEALS TO THE SENSES

USE WRITING THAT APPEALS TO THE SENSES TO GOOD
EFFECT IN SCENES.

■ IMAGES AS FOCUSING ELEMENTS
■ USES OF STATIC SCENES
■ EXERCISES

Images as focusing elements

Good writing appeals to the senses, and this can be used to
great effect in scenes. Sometimes the images in a scene center
the event.

Mary Morris always uses the senses to push emotional awareness in her fiction and nonfiction. In *Nothing to Declare:
Memoirs of a Woman Traveling Alone,* she pulls the reader deep into
exotic Mexico, painting picture after picture with language that
is at once lush and precise. In the chapter from which this passage is excerpted, she tells about her visit to Palenque with a
friend, and, later, their visit to the waterfalls and cool pools of
Agua Azul. One of the first things she notes, in the wooden dressing room, is: "A dead tarantula lay on the floor." She goes on to
swim. A young boy enters the pool and swims beside her; he is
not a very good swimmer, "flailing about like a puppy," and the
current is strong. In a little while she gets out to eat, and when

her friend, looking beyond her toward the pool, registers horror on her face, the narrator looks back to the pool, too.

> From the corner of my eye I saw the boy who had been swimming next to me. He seemed to be riding one of those carnival watersled rides because he was practically sitting up and the current was just taking him along. I could see his face now and he looked familiar to me, like an old acquaintance you meet after many years but cannot quite place.
>
> He was silent. This is what I remember most. The silence. He never screamed or shouted or cried for help. His face had the concentration of a good student taking an important exam. When he got to the falls, he twisted his body, trying to grab onto a branch, and then he was gone without a sound. Suddenly we were both screaming and pointing at nothing, at nothing at all except the rush of water.

Although Morris emphasizes the silence of the event—an eerie commentary that takes in her sense of impotence and the boy's helplessness, as well as the Mexican sense of fate—it is the vividness of the pictures she paints that carries the horror of the scene. We see the fierce water, the boy's face, the twisting of his body. It's like a very fast slide show. A little later in the chapter, she comments on the men in the search party, with "bodies so perfect and beautiful that I wanted to touch them as they bent over the water and put their faces in, like divers after mother-of-pearl." This contrast to the twisting body of the boy going over the falls is a terrible observation, one that brings home in an unexpected, memorable way what is lost.

Let's look at a vignette that is oblique, pithy, and disturbing. The central event: The narrator slept with her sister's husband. The narrator reflects on what he said to her, but the real heart of the scene is in its description, which carries great emotional content. On first glance, the passage may appear to be narrative summary, but when you read it you realize that you know where the tryst occurred, some of what was said, and, most of all, the narrator's acute consciousness of place, that place becoming a part of the erotic memory. This scene is from a story, "Festival," by Victoria Lancelotta.

> My sister's husband, the first time we were together, said to me, *She told me the two of you were the same.* He wrapped his hands in my hair, darker than hers and never quite as long, and pulled until my head rocked back, until I thought my breath would stop. He licked the sweat that slicked my throat and ran between my breasts. We were in my bedroom which was hot and oven-close, windows facing an alley, the back lot of a church. There was a festival, the bingo hall, the wheel of fortune, the priests who sat at paper-covered tables and ate sausage wrapped in dripping napkins and foil. There were the smells of grilling meat and fried dough, burnt sugar, sweat and sweet perfume.
>
> My sister's husband told me things about her I already knew. He told me he loved her and he told me how much.

Note that there are action beats that are spelled out: Her sister's husband speaks to her, pulls her hair, licks her, tells her more things about her sister. The power of the scene, however, is in the way the narrator conveys her intense awareness of sensory impressions, conveying through them the eroticism of the event. The "fire" of the relationship is conveyed by the description of things. The displacement of emotion can be very powerful.

Kate Wheeler, once ordained a Buddhist nun in Burma and later ordained a "best young American novelist" by *Granta,* wrote a collection of stories called *not where i started from.* There's lots of cultural dislocation, lots of journeying toward enlightenment, lots of humor, mischief, sorrow, and irony in these stories— and lots of memorable settings and sensory experiences. In her story "Ringworm," a young woman is recounting her stay in the

Pingyan Monastery in Burma, where she contracted ringworm. In one scene, she tells about a tall nun treating her with a cylinder of rolled leaves:

> Cradling my head, Nandasayee now rubbed the leaves onto the ringworm, carefully following its outline counterclockwise. This stung a little. Later I learned that the leaves were from a hot pepper bush. Her finger pads were slightly moist and soft, like frogs' palps. I could smell the green crushed leaf, and her body, scorched where mine was sharp.
>
> This would cure me of anything, I thought. I'd been there six months then, physically touched by no one.

What is wonderful about Wheeler's writing is that the lush descriptions are all so integrated into the actions of the stories. Note, too, how her response to the ministrations of the nun reveals to us that she has been without physical contact, and has felt the loss terribly.

Another very sensual writer is Rosa Shand, author of a novel, *The Gravity of Sunlight,* about an American couple living in 1970s Uganda. In the following short scene, a fragmentary transition between two other scenes, Shand basically flashes three images: Agnes giving snacks to children (notice the colors); Agnes's appearance (the color carries over here); the African women on her porch.

> She splashed grape juice in the cups. The drink spread a blue mustache as far as Lulu's cheeks. A sticky-fingered hand came up at her. She poked a cookie at it, and then at another and another.
>
> "Hodi." The call was from the front. It said somebody'd come. She was quite unhideable, with all the kafuffle with the children. Their sorry Peugeot you heard miles away had announced she was at home.
>
> "Karibu," she yelled back. That said, All right, come in, since you know I'm home and I have no escape.

Her hands were purple and most of her hair had pulled loose from her plait and flew out in all directions, but her smile turned bona fide. Two women—Baganda women, dressed in bright *basutis*—stood on her front porch.

Shand's novel is drenched in colors, heat, sounds, smells—the African atmosphere. The sensory experiences of Africa change the protagonist.

In her collection *The Red Passport,* Katherine Shonk writes about post-Communist Russia, startling the reader with the disconcerting combination of exoticism and familiarity. The story "Kitchen Friends" opens "On a high-ozone morning in Moscow, midsummer 1996 . . ." at the moment of an explosion, while the POV character, Leslie, is waiting for a trolleybus. In this brief excerpt, slightly into that event, see how she paints a vivid picture of the aftermath and the people in it.

All around Leslie, people began to lurch up from the earth, arms spread wide, like children imitating flowers in a school play. Wait for me, Leslie thought. Surveying her arms and legs, she found her limbs intact. Slowly she rose, a tender shoot blossoming to full height. Pulling loose from the street, she faced the bus and took her first steps on this new, wondrous earth.

Smoke-charred passengers clambered from the rear of the bus, arms flapping wildly. As they staggered away, cleaner passersby and would-be riders descended upon them. A young man in a red blazer chased a woman with charcoal handprints on her face, her skirt ripped to her waist. Only a few people lay bleeding on the ground, tended by police. Several women sat weeping on the curb, rubbing their eyes with dirty knuckles, while others muttered to themselves and wandered close to the traffic. Men took off their soiled shirts and strutted around the crumbled carcass of the trolleybus, gesturing and pointing.

Leslie draped her arm around one of the wandering women and told her not worry. "I can't hear! I've gone deaf!" the woman shouted . . .

If you find yourself stopping the action or delaying it in order to describe setting or characters, you should study published authors whose work can teach you that "description" isn't a discrete element in narrative. Think of the Navajo mysteries of Tony Hillerman. The evocation of the reservation landscape is essential to plot, where the mystery is tied up with the culture and those who have shattered its ways. Watch how Hillerman paints his portrait of place for you by the way people move in it.

Forget those high school classes where you talked plot, setting, character, theme. Those things aren't separate! You want your description to exist as part of action and emotion, part of the meaning of your scenes. Look for this blending in everything you read. You'll soon be able to spot the writers who "stop and start" and the ones who integrate description—make it a part of the flow of the action of the scene—and I feel certain you will have an appreciation for the latter. Sometimes, in fact, an awe.

Sentence elaboration

To get the hang of composing vividly sensual scenes, try starting with simple sentences that capture a moment in the action of a scene, or a caught emotion, and then expand upon it with rich sensory details.

When Erin McGraw wants to drive home just how true it is that her main character in "Ax of the Apostles," a priest, is hungry, she doesn't say, "He was terribly hungry all the time." She writes a paragraph that leaves no doubt of his suffering.

The passage: His hunger was becoming a kind of insanity. Food never left his mind; when he taught, he fingered the soft chocolates in his pocket, and at meals he planned his next meal. Nightly he ate directly from the refrigerator, shoveling fingerfuls of leftover casserole into his mouth, wolfing slice after slice of white bread. He dunked cold potatoes through the gravy's mantle of congealed fat, scooped up leathery cheese sauce. He ate as if he meant to disgust himself, but his disgust wasn't enough to stop him. Instead, he awakened deep in the night, his stomach blazing with indigestion, and padded back to the kitchen for more food.

Let's try a few more:

The sentence: The day was gloomy.
The passage: We woke to a gray sky, as if a great comforter hung over us. The house felt claustrophic. I turned on all the lamps, but found myself standing at the window staring out. I couldn't shake the feeling that the weather would never change, that I would never feel cheerful again. There was nothing I wanted to do but go back to bed.

The sentence: The wind blew.
The passage: A low dry wind gust came up, gritty and gray as powdered gravel. A fierce small dust devil, whirling like a baby twister, roared over them.

The sentence: Hollis was a good dancer.
The passage: Hollis had a routine all worked out. He almost stood in place, with a shuffle stomp stomp, shuffle stomp stomp, but was easy to dance with because he was so good with his arms. He nudged and tugged, and sent a girl out to be reeled back in.

In some ways, this whole chapter has been a reiteration of that old saw: Make your writing vivid, show, don't tell. It's about narrative with detail. But keep in mind that you want details to be part of action, not tacked on for effect. And do remember to engage all of the reader's senses, not just sight. In my novel *A Chance to See Egypt* there is a scene where Divina, a village girl in Mexico, prepares a meal for the protagonist, Riley. I wanted the scene to be deeply *felt* by Riley, in a literal way. He helps Divina eviscerate the birds that she will cook. She says that they will wash, and then she says, "Give me your hands."

> She scooped water from the bucket and poured it over his hands again and again until the water ran clean from his fingers. The water was cool. She gently rubbed her finger across his cuticles, turned his hands, and wiped the palms. She took the bowl away and set the bucket aside. She took a cloth from a stool by the door and carefully dried his hands, then her own.
>
> His heart was pounding.

How simple the event is: A woman washes a man's hands.

Sometimes a writer's style is lean, dry, with little embellishment. If you think you want to write like that, you might take a look at Amy Hempel, Ana Consuelo Matiella, Paula Fox, Elena Lappin, Kate Walbert, Abigail Thomas, Albert Camus, and other writers whose work lies sparingly on the page. Look at your own work and see what words you can do without.

A special case: scenes without event

> A static scene: Sometimes a passage is used that establishes elements of scene, but that lacks event. A static scene has a function, but should be used with caution.

Earlier I mentioned that sometimes an author employs elements of scene to establish ambience, character, even aspects of plot, but does so without building an event. Such passages do not meet the criteria I listed earlier for scenes, but they do have functions in stories. You want to know when you are doing this, because you don't want such a passage to fill the space you thought was moving your story. First of all, "scenic scenes" have to be very good indeed to keep our attention; they run the risk of being skip-overs. Second, if you don't know this is what you're doing, then you're not paying attention to the basic scene principles, and your scenes won't be doing the work you want them to do to move your story.

In most stories, stand-alone scenic passages are fairly rare, but I have chosen some text from Ron Hansen's famous novel *Mariette in Ecstasy* because he is so good at using both scenes and imagistic passages to good effect. I have numbered the paragraphs so that you can look to them as I discuss them.

The novel was very popular for three reasons. First, Hansen's lyrical, vivid prose was mesmerizing, a joy to read. Second, readers loved the feeling that they were getting an inside look at the secret lives of contemplative nuns. Third, the story line itself was intriguing, and readers have always been drawn to stories about miracles, visions, stigmatas, and so on if they are presented in a readable way. Hansen managed to give the reader a considerable amount of information while maintaining a through-line of tension: Will Mariette be accepted by the nuns into the life of the convent? Will her religious raptures be proven true or false? Even in so short a passage as I present below, you can see something of the strategy he used to do this.

1. Everyone is in her pew seat and contemplating the high altar behind the oakwood grille. Sister Léocadie goes immediately to Mother Saint-Raphaël, the former prioress and now mistress of novices, kneeling just before her and kissing Mother's pew railing as she confesses her lateness and penitence. Mother Saint-Raphaël gives the novice an irritated nod but no penance, so Sister Léocadie prostrates herself facedown on the floor until her shame has passed.

2. The prioress stands up and says, "We shall pray now for our new postulant." She kneels and so do thirty-one nuns. Everyone is upright on the kneeler, getting no support from

the pew, her hands in prayer just below her chin. When there is pain each will offer it up for the wretched souls in purgatory whose sins have kept them farthest from God.

3. Henri Marriott recites vesting prayers in the priest's sacristy as he turns up the hem of the ironed white alb that Sister Catherine has laid out and socks his hands into great sleeves that are as needleworked as doilies. With pain he ducks his head inside the alb and wriggles it over himself like a nightshirt. His strict precise Latin ticks from his mouth as he rectifies the hem of his shoes and ties the white rope cincture at his waist. Mademoiselle Baptiste, he thinks, and then scowls at Sister Catherine's uncertain writing on the intentions card for the Solemnity and tries to remember the girl's Christian name. Mariette Baptiste.

4. She is upstairs in a great country house and sitting at a Duchess desk in a pink satin nightgown as she pens instructions to the housemaid, saying to whom her jewelry and porcelains and laces and gowns ought to go.

She then stands and unties the strings at her neck so that the pink satin seeps onto a green Chinese carpet that is as plush as grass. And she is held inside an upright floor mirror, pretty and naked and seventeen. She skeins her chocolate-brown hair. She pouts her mouth. She esteems her full breasts as she has seen men esteem them. She haunts her milk-white skin with her hands.

Even this I give you.

5. Dr. Claude Baptiste stands at a kitchen window in red silk pajamas, drinking chickory in the sunrise, looking outside as if his hate were there, hearing Mariette just above him.

Chapter break
I have omitted Mariette's invitation to her wedding to Jesus.

6. Mixt.* Café au lait and a hunk of black bread that Sister Ange soaks in her great coffee bowl before she toothlessly chews. Sister Saint-Denis squashes her left forefinger down on the white tablecloth and sucks the dark crumbs from it.

7. And then work.

8. White sunlight and a wide green hayfield that languidly undulates under the wind. Eight sisters in gray habits surge through high timothy grass that suddenly folds against the ringing blades of their scythes. Mother Céline stoops and shocks the hay with twine and sun-pinked hands.

9. Four novices stand taciturnly at a great scullery table plucking tan feathers from twenty wild quail shot by a Catholic men's club just yesterday. Horseflies are alighting and tasting the skins, or tracing signatures in the hot air.

10. Sister Marguerite is in the scriptorium at a twelve-person library table, squinting at a text and then scratching a pen across a coarse sheet of paper as she translates into English *The Constitution of the Second Order of the Sisters of the Crucifixion in Accordance with the Common Observance of the Rule of Saint Benedict*. She tries a sentence to herself and writes, "When there is nothing else which we ought to be doing, it is our sweet obligation to pray."

11. Extern Sister Anne is still huffing breathlessly in the campanile as she grins up at the pigeons shuffling along the rafters and frantically jerking their heads toward her. She gets a handful of sweet-corn kernels from her gray habit's pocket and scatters them on the flooring, and the pigeons heavily flap down and trundle around her sandals. She then

---

* "Mixt" is the time to eat before work.

reads the time on her late husband's railway watch and grabs the chime pulls with hard brutal hands, heartily summoning her sisters to the hour of Terce and High Mass.

12. White cottages and a shaggy dog tucking its nose in four parts of a juniper hedge and then trotting on. Chimes for High Mass are ringing at a great distance and a girl is eating toast on a milking stool outside the general store. She glances up the road, sucking jam from her thumb, and gets to her knees on the green porch.

13. Mariette Baptiste is in solemn procession to the Church of Our Lady of Sorrows in her mother's wedding trousseau of white Holland cloth and watered silk. Trailing the postulant on horseback or phaetons and carriages are girlfriends and high school classmates and villagers.

Dr. Baptiste is not present.

She has hoped for an hour's peace and contemplation on the way to the church, but she is blessed or praised or spoken to by a hundred people and she is given pink and white nasturtiums wrapped in a flute of parlor wallpaper. She thanks the people by smiling or touching their wrists or fleetingly laying her hand on a baby's head.

14. —Were you happy to have so much attention?

—Well, no. I had been hoping to present myself to the sisters with Christ's own plainness and humility.

—But you got instead a pageant.

—Yes.

—And you thought your sisters were passing harsh judgment?

—Even then.

Discussion

1. In this paragraph, the author describes a typical incident in the life of the convent—the imposition of a penance for a sister's

lateness. This occurs early on, and it helps the reader be drawn into the world of the novel, and the world Mariette is entering.

2. Again, we are getting a little lesson on how things are in the convent. Obviously we need to know these practices in order to understand Mariette's life there. Reread the first two paragraphs to see how you have a picture of the nuns in place in the chapel.

3. Here the author is giving us a moment in the rituals connected to receiving Mariette into the convent; the priest is preparing for her service, and this is part of the story and necessary to the plot. At the same time, the reader is given a nice description of the priest's costume, and a relationship is mentioned that will come up again.

4. What a gorgeous paragraph this is and how much it accomplishes! We are given the beautiful seventeen-year-old Mariette on her last day at home. Note the sensual details of her surroundings, and of her body. This is, of course, also part of the story line.

5. "as if his hate were there . . ." The author slips in a single word, *hate,* to alert us to the attitude of Mariette's father toward her entering the convent, and gives us a snapshot of him. Nothing happens, but we need this moment. His character is crucial to the story.

6. These wonderful women are introduced to us. They will be part of Mariette's community. There is no event, no real scene, but this is further preparation for the reader of the girl's new life.

7. "And then work." Because of course that is an integral part of every day. This is information, pure and simple, and yet it is conveyed as the ultimate compression of scenes that we know go on.

8. And here is one of them. List the describing words in this beautiful paragraph. Then read it again and note how they are used to convey motion, action, life.

9. The work of the kitchen. Hansen must have had divine guidance to come up with these moments. Static scenes indeed! Horseflies lighting, novices plucking: They do not add up to "event," but they do expand the work mentioned in number 7.

10. This static scene not only lets us see a different kind of work, and a different layer of nunhood, but it also opens onto one of the rules that guide the contemplative life.

11. Note in this paragraph the clear beats of action. Understand that all of this is part of the world of the novel, but these little scenes are not "events" in the sense that we have discussed them in scenes. Still, they are essential to the development of the novel, for the reasons I discussed above.

12. Now we enter the actual plot line, the movement of Mariette from home to convent. The girl sees her coming. This is a small event and a transition into the story line.

13. We have been prepared by number 12 for this small scene of Mariette's passing on the way to her big day, when she is accepted into the community as a postulant. Her father is absent. And we are told what she is thinking.

14. Now we jump ahead, an interesting strategy of the author's. He inserts this moment of inquiry, which will come much later in chronology, about her experiences as she enters the convent, about her decisions, her ecstasies, the visitations of the stigmata, etc. This one, with its little arc, is about the passage through town, illuminated in the previous passage. This dialogue is, in effect, an excerpt of a much larger, longer scene, and we dip into it numerous times throughout the novel. It is a perfect example of the kind of "ghost" scene to which I referred several times—one that occurs whole in the mind of the author and the experience of the characters, and, ultimately, in the mind of the reader.

You would learn a lot from reading *Mariette in Ecstasy* and noting which scenes are the ones that build the plot—Mariette's growing religious rapture, the mixed responses of the sisters in her community, the questioning by her superiors, and so on. Read them with the principles that you have been studying in mind, and then see how the author embeds the story elements in lyrical prose.

Now, a last word about images. For some, it's definitely not the way to go. Elmore Leonard has made a career of writing lively fiction while eschewing images and adverbs (by his own account). Other writers also prefer the crispness or leanness or transparency of spare prose. No one can tell you what's right for you. If you want to enrich your stories, though, you can create images in many ways—including using concrete details that seem the opposite of lush. And if you do prefer the beauty of thickly descriptive prose, don't lose track of your story line.

Exercises

• **Sensory Observation:** Think of an action that has strong emotional undercurrents, and write two or three moments in it. Then list the sensory elements of the setting that the narrator notices as the actions occur. Now write the scene more fully. In a first-person POV, the narrator looks to the surroundings to project deep emotions. Some suggestions:

    a. A couple quarreling while they are in a wilderness setting

    b. Children playing in the yard while adults are having coffee on the porch, after a funeral (Try it with an adult narrator; then try a child's POV.)

c. A parent and child or children engaged in something like fishing, target shooting, or another sport

Remember that it isn't necessary to write heavy description. The emphasis is on concrete details.

• *Elaborating Sentences:* Take a simple sentence of action and write a paragraph that provides a richness of concrete detail to show the meaning of the sentence. Examples:

a. He was afraid of the dark.
b. He fell and assessed the damage.
c. The men looked me over.
d. She was cleaning the birds.

You can also look at passages and reduce them to simple sentences of action. Working backward in this way, you study how an author created a richly descriptive scene. If you are working in a group, you could trade passages and sentences.

• *A Deeply Felt Activity:* Think of an ordinary activity undertaken by a character or characters, and infuse it with sensory richness. Make one element more important than the others, but include more than one sensory awareness. Think of the emotion conveyed by the images. This exercise contrasts with the first one, which asked you to have a narrator project emotions onto things outside the self. Here, you should have the POV character deeply engaged in the activity, experiencing it sensually. You have wide latitude in your choice of subject matter. Chopping wood, making love, diapering a baby, writing a letter, preparing a meal: One activity is not inherently more dramatic or meaningful than another.

• *The Primary Image:* Instead of starting with a character, start with an image. Locate yourself in a setting that interests you, perhaps someplace you have traveled, or would like to travel, or a place that scares you, or thrills you. Identify something in the setting that evokes a response in *you*. Write freely for five minutes about that image. Now imagine a character in that setting confronting that same *something,* and having a reaction. Will the character be engaged in an activity that draws attention to the image you have in mind? Or will the image be a distraction? Or will it be a projection of something emotional in the character? You have many possibilities, but begin with the image.

PART THREE

SOME USEFUL SCENE SKILLS

9

SCENE ACTIVITY AND
CHARACTER RESPONSE

MAKE YOUR WRITING INTERESTING BY DRESSING SCENES
WITH ACTIVITY.

LEARN HOW TO BALANCE THE RESPONSES OF CHARACTERS
TO THE ACTIONS OF A SCENE.

- How DOES *activity* DIFFER FROM *action*?
- WHAT IS *grounding*?
- EXERCISES

Dressing scenes with activity

Activity is made up of incidental motions that help to build
meaning in small units by amplifying the larger actions or
character qualities.

A common problem in early drafts of scenes is the absence of
what we call *grounding:* those details that tell us where we
are and what is going on around the events in the scene. Think
of it as letting us live in the scene.

I recently read a student scene that opened on people talking
about something urgent. After two pages, the scene ended: "Then
he stalked out, leaving her heartbroken."

Stalked out of where? There had not been a mention of the
room. They might have been sitting, standing, walking, or
floating, for all the reader knew from the passage. The writer

left the reader with no picture in mind of the abandoned character.

A good scene lets us know the spatial relationships of people and things. Are characters near one another? Is one avoiding the other by standing behind a chair, or staying busy to avoid contact? What happens in a tense altercation if one character is holding a cat in her lap and the other character moves fast enough to nearly knock over a lamp? And why have you put them in a room instead of outside, by the shed? Or in the produce section of a grocery store, where the scene might take place with tightly controlled dialogue but end with a squished tomato?

The incidental movements and activities of characters help to define them, and the things they surround themselves with and use are part of who they are. Besides that, what they do in response to events can be "external signs of what they are feeling."

Filling the *activity* of scenes requires a large reservoir of images in your mind. You must get off your feet, out of your house, and around people. What you visualize in your imagination has to draw on real things you have seen. If you haven't seen something to build on, you will inevitably draw on clichés, such as movies, other people's writings, or the same-old-same-old things you have written before.

Observe the differences in how people move, given the variations in their height, weight, age, and gender. Watch children of all ages. Note the ways that people express distress, pleasure, boredom, curiosity. Pay attention to what people have in their rooms, and how objects are used. This is the stuff that becomes part of the tiny details of your writing that makes it vivid, specific, and authentic, and uniquely your own voice. If you look at writers' published journals, you will find many observations of incidental behaviors that intrigued the writer. Start your own such list. I have seen the writer Mary Morris generously share a sample journal from the many she has developed over her years of travel, study, and writing. She carries one with her everywhere. She is constantly observing and recording the world around her, and when she sits down to write, she has not only her imagination but a keen record to draw from, and it shows in the rich details of her stories. I've also heard Richard Ford say that he collects snippets from newspapers and magazines, and little pieces of paper on which he has recorded quick observations, letting them pile up until the mass seems to cry out to him that he has something he needs to write. I do something similar, stuffing notions in a shoebox, knowing that my aging mind is a sieve!

If you are writing something that has an unfamiliar world of its own, such as a work setting or a foreign locale, it is especially important to become familiar with the stuff of that world. I recently read *War by Candlelight,* the debut collection of stories by Daniel Alarcon. Alarcon was Peruvian born but raised in the United States. After his college days, he went back to Peru on a Fulbright and lived in a barrio. It certainly shows in the richly textured details of his stories, where clowns beg on buses, packs of kids roam the streets at night, and plastic balls ricochet off the iron bars on windows.

When I wrote *A Chance to See Egypt,* about a Chicago widower who goes to Mexico and falls in love again, I chose an area where lots of seniors visit or retire—the Chapala region near Guadalajara. I flew there to visit Chapala and nearby villages, to sit in the squares, poke about in markets, and peek into churches. For settings of other books, I have attended special-interest groups, visited regional museums, talked to elders in retirement centers, read dozens of books and perused hundreds of photographs, learned to line dance, interviewed sixth-grade boys, scanned old yearbooks, chosen somebody's living room as a character's own; I've looked and listened.

In early drafts, my scenes are often fairly spare, and I try to enrich them in revision. An interaction of the function of the scene and one's style influences the choices of how much and what kinds of details to use. Read other writers and take special note of this aspect of their writing. The last thing you want is a scene stuffed with useless details.

In brief, consider these factors:

• Small descriptions and activities establish settings and tone for the scene. Sometimes a few lines are enough. Sometimes more is needed, especially if the setting is exotic.

• Small movements can provide beats that give moments of rest or emphasis in an exchange of dialogue. Again, you will learn this by studying other writers.

• Movements can be used to express the emotional response of a character, either during the scene or as a sustained reaction at the end.

Examples

Let's look at a few passages that nicely illustrate my maxims.

Elizabeth Berg's novel *Durable Goods* is written in the voice of an adolescent girl getting through a hot summer after her mother's death. Here the narrator is with her sister.

> One evening after dishes, Diane comes into my room. "What's up?" she asks.
>
> "What do you mean?"
>
> She holds up my bottle of Evening in Paris, checks the level, puts it carefully back down in place. "How come you're all alone?"
>
> "I'm doing my homework."
>
> "I mean alone all the time. Are you fighting with Cheryl-anne?"
>
> "I don't know. She is."
>
> "How come?"
>
> "She's just that way sometimes. She just is. She's not my only friend."
>
> I am hoping Diane doesn't ask for a list of others. She doesn't. She stretches out on my bed. "Ummm," she says. "You have a good bed."

I get up from my desk, sit down beside her.

"Diane?"

"Yeah?"

"Do you ever think about leaving, about running away?"

"What happened?"

"Nothing. I just . . . Nothing happened. I just think sometimes I'd like to live somewhere else."

There is a shift in her face. "Where you're not a punching bag, huh?"

It is too bold, how she does it. It is too much out.

"I don't know, I mean just . . . I think I would just like to leave, that's all. Go somewhere else."

"Without Dad."

"Well, yeah. I think he likes it here."

Diane's laugh is like a short cry. "I don't. I don't think he likes it anywhere."

"If you asked Dickie, would he take you away?"

Diane stands up, goes over to my window. "If I asked Dickie to do anything, he would do it." Her back is to me. The truth of what she is saying is in the line of her spine: she stands tall with it. Then she turns around, a half smile on her face. "Why? You want to come?"

You can sense the unspoken tension in this scene: the references to the abuse by the father, to the escape of the big sister to her boyfriend's arms, the sadness and pain of the narrator's loneliness during this summer of change. Diane's handling of her sister's perfume bottle establishes their intimacy—and delays the hard question she asks. If you read this short scene aloud (actually the passage ends before the scene is over) you will see the room and sense the underlying emotion. The event is the conversation, the sharing of the despair; the small actions contribute to it.

In Aaron Hamburger's story "A Man of the Country," 1990s post–Cold War Prague comes to life. The narrator is going home with "Jirka the giant," who has taken time off from work in honor of the narrator's departure.

> We turn right onto Malostranske namesti and Jirka puts his hand on my neck. His touch feels cold and heavy, like a metal clamp. "Please, my friend." He slips his whole arm around my shoulders and pulls me against his hip. I try not to get hard because we've never talked about it openly, this propensity of mine to be attracted to him.
>
> Three teenage boys dressed in oversized sweatshirts and backwards baseball caps like the hip-hop artists they watch on Euro MTV are heading straight for us, but Jirka doesn't drop his arm. He points at the show window of a store that imports Levi's. "It is funny *reklama* for slips. How you say *reklama*?"
>
> "Advertisement." The ad in question, for men's underwear by Diesel, consists of three close-up shots of crotches in various states of arousal as seen through white briefs. The word for underwear in Czech is *slip*. "What kind of *slip* do you wear?"
>
> Jirka hikes down the waist of his pants low enough for me to see his paisley-print bikini briefs.
>
> The boys walk by and take no notice of us.

Now, what has happened in this short scene? A flirtation. An opening in the window of seduction. Only instead of in a bedroom, or on a couch at home, the writer puts these two young men on the streets of Prague, crossing a bridge and walking past a store window, in full view of kids who might notice what is going on between them. The details are fully a part of the event, aren't they? And they are interesting to us American readers, right down to the Czech word for *underwear*.

Here is a scene composed by apprentice writer Gleam Powell in a workshop. She wrote it as an exercise exploring tension between two characters that surfaces while they are engaged in an activity together. Note that she chose to have the characters step back rather than enter a full confrontation, but she makes it clear that there's something bubbling between these sisters after their mother's death. Their history provides "combustion" between them, a source of the tension that underlies their surface politeness. They get around their quarrel by focusing on the domestic task at hand.

Elizabeth flung the dishtowel over the bottom of another white china plate, swiping it quickly. "There, that should be the last of the good china."

"Where do you suppose these glasses go?" Mary opened a cupboard door and glanced at the row of red and white soup cans and shut it. "Not there."

"Look in the dining room. There's a cabinet full of good crystal," Elizabeth said.

Mary walked into the dining room, a long oblong of a room with a dark red and blue Turkish rug beneath a carved mahogany table. Eight chairs sat in place at the table, their seats covered with a shiny burgundy and gold satin. A spiral arrangement of tall white lilies lit up the darkened room. Their sweet perfume choked Mary, and she cleared her throat before she spoke.

"Yes, here it is," she said. "Here's where they belong." She walked back to the kitchen and picked up four pieces of the fragile glass stems, two in each hand.

"Careful," Elizabeth said. "Don't try to carry too many at once."

"I think I can handle it," Mary said, trying to keep her voice pleasant.

"If they chip, they're really hard to replace."

"Elizabeth, I can do this. I'm grown up now. I'm just not familiar with where everything belongs." Mary turned and faced her sister, her hands on her hips.

"That's true. You haven't been around much these last few years." Elizabeth leaned over the lilies and removed a few stray pieces of yellow pollen from the table, pinching them tightly in her fingers.

Mary slammed shut a cupboard door. The crystal glasses clinked against one another. "I was teaching halfway around the world. Mother understood that."

"Where's that big pink bowl we used for the crab salad? Haven't we washed that?"

"Elizabeth, Mother understood."

"There it is. There's that bowl." Elizabeth grabbed the pink dish and carried it into the kitchen.

Mary leaned against the cupboard and shook her head. She took a deep breath and followed Elizabeth into the kitchen. "Look, it's getting late. How about we get into Ollie Jones's rice and chicken casserole."

Elizabeth nodded. "Good idea. I'll light the oven." She didn't look back at Mary. She walked over to the oven. "350 ought to do it."

In that scene you saw just what I was talking about earlier, in chapter 6, "Tension": a decision on the part of the characters not to clash about unspoken issues—who had been taking care of Mother, who has "seniority" in the relationship, and so on. Instead, they found plenty right in front of them to disagree about, and then Mary made a grown-up decision to keep the peace. You also see how *activity* is used to dispel that tension in a way that shows us how these women live.

A caveat: If you give your readers so much description of activity that it gets in the way of real action and it interrupts dialogue too much, you will have defeated your purpose, which is to sweep up the reader into the story.

How much is enough or too much? Unfortunately, I can't give you a formula. I can say:

• Give your readers enough details of activity that they are able to picture the setting and event, but don't overdescribe so that they have no imaginative work to do.

• Don't emphasize characters that aren't important to the scene.

• Use activity to introduce rhythm to your dialogue, but don't make the lines stutter with unnecessary interruptions, and don't belabor incidentals that make the reader lose the thread.

• Leave out the obvious stuff, the movements that come to mind too quickly (characters gazing out the window or crossing their legs); your actions should be fresh and distinct.

• Ask yourself what purpose your beats of activity have served. Did they supply information? Build tension? Provide relief?

Exercises

• *Integrated Activity:* Write a scene in which a character is under pressure that stresses him while he has to perform an activity that requires concentration. The pressure comes from something that is related to the present activity. A character might be loading a truck with stolen goods, or cleaning out the room of a person who has abandoned the family, committed a crime, or died.

• *Peripheral Activity:* Write a scene in which the activity of characters is incidental to the real purpose or subject of the interaction. For example, a woman cooks dinner while her husband sits at the table paying bills; they talk about their wayward teenager. In another example, kids are decorating a gym for a dance while a conflict builds about who did what or who likes whom. In this case, the talk will have some elements of the activity ("Here, hold this—") but the subtext should emerge.

• *Smart Story:* Readers love stories and passages that allow them a peek into a world they know little about. If you are lucky enough to have an insider's knowledge of an interesting subject—some aspect of medicine, something in the natural world, in the arts, etc.—create a scene set in a situation that uses that knowledge, even though it isn't the subject or pulse of the scene. Alternatively, pick something you are interested in and learn enough about it for one scene. You could do any of the scenes in this book, just set them in Antarctica! Or a dance company. An operating room. A cockpit. The writer Andrea Barrett had been published but she didn't really find her voice until she started writing about scientists, whereupon she won the National Book Award and other honors.

Remember, something has to make your writing stand apart from everyone else's. Could the intriguing fictional world you create be the key to your success?

Balancing action and response

Choose a scene you admire. Ideally, type it out so that you process it more attentively than as a reader. Now go through the scene and see how each of these components is developed or used (not all will be) in the scene. You have a wide range of choices in showing a character's response to the scene event(s):

1. Action: What happens? Is it *large* action or *small*?
2. Reflection of a character about an aspect of what is happening
3. Reflection of a character about an aspect of the past that is relevant
4. Expression of #2 or #3 in dialogue
5. Response of a character, interior, that feels immediate—*I am feeling this right now*—rather than reflective—*this is what I think of that*
6. An interior emotional response that leaks or bursts into an

action (also, look for small activity as a projection of feelings)

7. An emotional response that leads a character to raise questions (aloud or to self), formulate new goals, initiate action, etc.

As you identify each of the different kinds of character response, you can practice writing it in your own scenes. It will seem artificial to be so deliberate in exercises, but the practice will give you a wider range of strategies in your writing.

Examples

Below is a simply constructed passage from my novel *More Than Allies*. Maggie is a young mother who is estranged from her husband, Mo. Maggie lives with her mother-in-law, Polly, and has two little kids, Jay, a fifth-grader, and Stevie (a girl), a toddler. This passage occurs soon after Polly informs Maggie that she is going to take in a foster baby with special needs; Maggie is quite affected by the idea of Polly shifting her attention from her grandchildren to a new child. She also just got off the phone from talking to Mo, who wants her to move to Texas, where he is working.

The structure: scene summary, scene summary, scene. By "scene summary" I mean that all the described action takes place close together in time—not last week or yesterday—but isn't spelled out in detail.

Notice in this scene that Maggie is, in effect, responding to everyone: to Mo, who just called; to Polly, who seems to be abandoning her (Maggie was once Polly's foster child herself); to her kids, who just woke up and need her. She hardly has time to think, but think she does.

In the first paragraph, the narration tells the reader straight out what is going on and what Maggie is thinking about and feeling. It's a bit of summary that leads you into the second paragraph, which is still compressed, and then to the dialogue that focuses on the immediacy of the scene. I have remarked on the scene in brackets, indicating the type of character responses. (Note: Gretchen is Polly's daughter and Maggie's friend.)

Jay stumbled out to eat cereal about nine, then went back to bed. Maggie looked to Polly for a hint of what to do with him, but Polly was writing out bills. Maggie had already had breakfast with her, and fed Stevie, and was finding it difficult to keep from brooding about Mo's phone call. She was relieved when Polly said she had to dig some things out of the garage to get ready for the new baby.

Polly brought in an old crib, and Maggie scrubbed it while Polly went off for a tin of paint. They moved it out onto the patio and painted it white with a turquoise trim. In a burst of creativity, Maggie drew tiny flowers on the headboard. [An interior emotional response that leaks into an action. She is trying to participate in Polly's pleasure and be a help to her.] She could feel Polly's pleasure and excitement building. Babies.

"What do you know about the baby?" she asked her.

Polly said she was the child of an addicted mother, and wasn't going to be easy at first. Maggie chewed on her lip. [Small action to project feeling] She could see it now: Polly rocking and walking an infant, Gretchen pouting and playing poor-me recluse, Maggie and her kids suddenly odd ones out. [Like much of the passage, a reflection about what is happening, but one that embraces problems she is having with Gretchen as well as her fears of losing Polly's support] Polly was humming to herself. The sunshine gleamed on her short black hair. "Kendra," she said.

Jay wandered out, still in his pj's, rubbing his eyes. He went straight to Polly for a hug, glowering at his mother. Maggie felt a twinge of envy and hurt. [Immediate interior response] "How about a real breakfast now?" she asked, trying to sound cheerful. She had read somewhere that if you refused to let your child cloud your spirits, he learned—what? She couldn't remember, and she couldn't imagine. She felt what he felt, not the other way around. He clung to Polly, who extricated herself and patted him on the back. "I've got a little more to do here, Jay-Jay, but you could fry some bacon if you like." Jay looked at his mother, his chin up.

"I'll make some cinnamon toast," Maggie said. "Stevie loves it." Stevie, hearing her name, ran across the patio and flung herself at Maggie.

Sometimes children are like great huge sacks of flour to be lugged and handled and lifted and kept. Sometimes Maggie would like to close her eyes and think there was nobody out there who needed her. [The kind of "overview" thinking that sometimes appears at the close of a scene; an overall response]

"I like it too," Jay said.

"Then why don't you help me make it?" Surely they could manage that. Making a mess was always therapeutic.

In the following scene from my novel *Plain Seeing,* the protagonist, Lucy, is on her way to see her lover. Lucy is married to the president of a college in a small town, and is the mother of a teenager. She makes a quick stop at the bank and encounters a woman from the college. Her reaction to the inconsequential meeting gives the reader a little insight into Lucy's state of mind—she has long since given up being "the good wife"—but the real purpose of the scene is to get her to the place where a dramatic event will occur that has repercussions over the next year.

The scene is made up of small, inconsequential actions except for the final beat, the accident, and of Lucy's reflections on her position in the community and in her own life. Even though the accident that happens to her isn't her fault, there is a sense of inevitability, as if she is wandering toward it in her aimlessness.

She walked toward the library, then turned to the bank. The intersection was as frantic as ever, with cars speeding, and too many entries into the street right at that corner. There was the bank, the turn from the library, the turn into another bank across the way, and the cross street. She stepped into the intersection and waited for a car to bother to stop, then carefully made her way, watching for the other lane. When would they ever get a light? [The first paragraph is simple action, set in the context of describing the setting. Lucy is cautious.]

The first person she saw in the bank was Mrs. Mason from the college admissions office. Mrs. Mason was one of those officious busybody types who had managed, over twenty-five years, to bloat her clerk's job to quasi-administrative status. She was the kind of woman who felt entitled. Seeing her was a cold reminder to Lucy that she was a kind of public property. [Reflection about her status as Gordon's wife] She nodded in the woman's general direction and stood at the counter, pretending she had slips to put in order before approaching a teller. All she really needed was a single withdrawal slip, but she made entries onto the calculator. She tapped in twenty-three, the number of years she had been married, and fourteen, the age of her daughter, and she wondered what the sum meant. Had she loved for thirty-seven years? Been loved that long? Had she given, or received, all she was entitled to? [At first her response is just avoidance, but then it becomes reflective about the past.]

Should she subtract her child from her marriage? Or add her to her life? And what should she make of a year with Andy? Or the year with Richard in California? [Reflection about her status as a wife—an unfaithful one—and a mother that implies her unhappiness]

"Hello, Lucy," Mrs. Mason said, scooting alongside her at the counter. "We missed you at the opening."

"Mrs. Mason," Lucy said. She had to think, what opening? Ah, the art building for which Gordon had campaigned for years. There would have been no benefit to Lucy standing beside him as he cut a ribbon. She hadn't attended an official function in years. She remembered the last occasion, a keynote address by a lesbian poet, the kickoff of Women's History Month. The poet's inflammatory remarks provoked several young men to catcalls and fist-thrusts from the back of the room. Gordon himself ushered them out of the room, his arms draped over their shoulders paternally. [Simple memory]

Mrs. Mason was holding a pink receipt in her hand, indicating that her own transaction was completed. Seeing this, Lucy instantly felt bolder. "There's bound to be another, isn't there?" she said. She smiled and moved past Mrs. Mason to stand in line. Mrs. Mason would make the most of Lucy's airy terseness back in Admissions, but Lucy had been civil, the extent of her official duties. Gordon had long ago settled for her self-sufficiency, in lieu of social partnership.

She laid her envelope down and gave the teller her withdrawal slip. She stuck her cash carelessly into her purse, tucked it over her shoulder, and picked up the envelope. It was ripping along one side.

At the door she blinked in the bright spring sunshine. If she turned right, she had three blocks to walk to Andy's but then she would have the five blocks back to her car to walk. She decided she would retrace her steps to the restaurant, get the car, and park near the apartment. She never got away as quickly as she meant to do. She stepped into the crosswalk. A couple of cars whizzed by and then there was, amazingly, an empty street. She started across. She heard her name called—"Lucy! Over here!"—and looked across to see Andy coming out of the camera shop. She heard someone call out, "Mother!" and thought it was Laurie. Pausing, she looked around just in time to see the car upon her. The driver, a young woman, was touching up her lipstick. Her neck was craned so she could look in the rearview mirror. She was driving too fast. Lucy froze, not that it mattered. [The beats of action don't allow time for response. This is important to the tension.]

Don't! Lucy cries. She is catapulted straight up into the bright light. Her purse pops open and bills fly above her, and Laurie's photographs fly, too, first up, then down, like leaflets from the sky, falling toward her, a beautiful shower of color and dazzling smile and wheat-white hair. [Here the voice has pulled back from the close POV as Lucy is thrown into the air by the impact of the car; there is no character response.]

In my memoir, *Occasions of Sin,* I used a lot of fragmentary scenes, calling on memories that weren't much more than images, almost snapshots of moments in my childhood that captured the feelings between my mother and me.

When I was nine, my family traveled from Texas to Ohio to visit Daddy's Yankee parents, and then on to Washington, D.C., to see his sister. I became acutely conscious of my mother's outsider position in the family, and I sided with her, while my "chubby, bespectacled, and newly confident" little sister "did no wrong" with Daddy's kin. The purpose of this scene fragment is simply to establish that closeness between my mother and me in the unkind territory of Daddy's folks. Notice that in the memoir the presentation of the image includes my memory of my worry about my mother's health and attitude. A memoir is, in part, retrospection.

... When we stopped for the night at a spindly house that said "ROOMS," Mother said she was too tired to eat and I stayed behind with her, though I was hungry. After the coast was clear, we went downstairs and up the street to a corner grocery and bought chocolate bars.

Back in the room we gobbled our candy and drank water from the spigot, laughing in happy conspiracy and escape. She combed my hair and plaited it, and then I begged to do hers.

I was gentle as I could be, seeing how thin her hair was at the crown. In the mirror she watched me. She took the brush and scooted over, patting the stool to make a place for me. Side by side we studied ourselves in the mirror. I saw that I was like her but not like her, too. My eyes were dark, my brows heavy, but I was delicate like her.

She brushed a finger along my cheekbones. I turned and put

my arms around her neck. She crooned something about sticking together, by now a familiar theme. She looked so tired all the time. I wished I knew how to make it better. I wanted to be her reason for keeping at it, her reason to believe in the future.

How can life go on if you don't think that it's worth living?

Note how the narrator's response to the mother's gentle touch is immediate and physical, the embrace; but it is followed by the narrator's reflection that raises questions about her mother's well-being, and asserts her own desire to make her mother's life better.

Now study scenes of your choice, and try the strategies for yourself. You might start with scenes you have already written, integrating one more response strategy in a revision. Even if it seems arbitrary, use the different response strategies in your scenes to see how differently they make a scene work, how they set it up for different actions to follow and different character interactions.

10

SCENE OPENINGS

ESTABLISHING SCENE ELEMENTS IN OPENING LINES

- WHAT ARE SOME STRATEGIES FOR OPENING A SCENE?
- EXERCISES
- A WORD ABOUT SCENE ENDINGS

Drawing the reader in

Think of your opening lines as the come-hither and the open door.

The opening line of a story or book is crucial, because it draws the reader in with a promise: This will be a good story. This is good writing. You're going to like this. And in a book's chapters, you once again establish your voice as one the reader wants to hear.

Set the scene so that we are not confused. You may be carrying over from a prior scene (not necessarily the one right before), and so this scene links to earlier action and lets us know that time has passed. This is often done by repeating a phrase or an image from the earlier scene.

Of course the scene may be entirely fresh action, requiring a more fundamental orientation, unless it is your strategy to keep the reader in suspense until the scene unfolds and reveals itself. (I don't advise too much of this for beginners.)

Some passages I have written as examples follow.

It is possible to pull the reader into the heart of the story, beginning in medias res without getting lost, if your opening lines offer enough details of situation, setting, and potential conflict.

I slid to my bottom on the ice. "So much for the Olympics," I said. A teenage girl flew by like an angel, laughing—not at me, I hoped. It was a beautiful day to be out on the pond, like skating in a glass of pure water under bright light.

Cate laughed and helped me up. "You know, the trouble with guys is they either get it right the first time or they don't do it at all. That's why love affairs are so damned hard. It takes trial and error. It takes a little humiliation."

The scene may be a new event with a link to the story's history, and you want to establish that by beginning with narrative about the past. Sometimes you can do this with a word or phrase or image repeated from an earlier scene, to jostle the reader's memory.

In this example, you are moving from *narrative summary* to *scene:*

By the time Teresa started school, she could read real books from the library, write little stories with bad spelling, and draw a map of Oklahoma with dots for the capital and her town. It wasn't that anyone had started out to teach her all that, it was that she was so demanding. Every time her mother, Rebecca, sat down for two minutes, Teresa was there with a book or ten questions or something she had drawn. It had just been easier to give her what she wanted, and it had been fun. After a while, it had been a source of pride, though Rebecca tried not to show it. She was afraid she'd puff Teresa up and make her a precious and lonely child. [Summary ends here.]

It was no surprise when Teresa came home from her first day of school fuming at the stupidity of it all. [Transition sentence] "They had a sheet of paper as big as a refrigerator in the front of the room, Mama," she said, "and it had about six words on it. That was what the teacher called reading!"

You may want to get into the scene quickly with a moment of orientation, such as:

> Commenting on some aspect of character, setting, or event before entering the scene; this can be terse or long.

Winter days in Portland were often drippy and dreary. Shannon, hurrying from the bus stop in the rain, couldn't help thinking this was one too many bad days in a long series of them. And then there was her mother, waiting at her window as if Shannon were a little kid who had strayed away after dark. Her mother waved vigorously, and Shannon hurried to her, wanting, despite everything, to love her.

> Or commenting on life in general as it is illustrated by what is about to follow.

I never thought my world would seem small; I always believed I would care about things like global warming and AIDS in Africa until the day I died. But that day is coming closer, and what I've learned is that old age and infirmity are like cataracts, they cloud your vision. You start looking inward, and there's a lot there to occupy your mind, if you still have one. So who cares what the outside world has going on?

This little test they want to give me is more bad news, and I'm not far gone enough not to know it. I'd love to tell the chirpy bitch what I think of it and see if that counts on the senility chart, but she's busy laying things out on her shiny table, bobbing her head up and down to smile at me; my meanness would just fly right by her. So I sit down, too, and try to calm myself, as if my score really matters. As if I could change anything by playing nice.

As you will see, these are not entirely discrete strategies, but I wanted to give you some words to put around approaches that you can watch for and try. The important thing is that good writers do not wander into scenes or tell us more than we need to know.

In drafting a scene or story, you may very well need to write far more than what will end up in your polished work. Do not feel self-conscious about that. The writing that doesn't show up later may have been the path you had to clear to get to the story. All of us have our times of writing too little or too much.

In summary, when entering scenes try to:
- come in out of narrative summary.
- link to a prior scene.
- begin in medias res.
- comment on character, setting, or event.
- comment on life in general as illustrated by the scene to come.
- open the scene, and then pause action for character musing that establishes tone or background. (Careful!)

Let's look at some more examples.

The first set are all from Alice Mattison's collection of "intersecting stories," *Men Giving Money, Women Yelling*. It's such an endearing, blithe book, it is easy to overlook how well it is crafted. She uses many different strategies to get into stories and scenes. Here are some *openings* into scenes from different Mattison stories. Just watch the way she gives the reader a little orientation and then begins each scene. The passages begin with a statement of "how things usually were," the *conditional*. I have marked the beginning of the scenes by underlining the first few words.

Try to identify the strategies she uses.

When it was time for him to go home, he leaned on the wall, talking. Kitty would stand opposite him, glancing at the door, his coat in her arms. "<u>But he's kind,</u>" said Ida, one night after he left. Martin had come for dinner and it had taken hours to get rid of him. It was a school night and Kitty had work to do.

"He sits there," Kitty said, "as if he's growing roots into the furniture. He likes me too much. I did get robbed that night. Martin robbed me."[*]

I'd just come to Rochester, the town where I grew up, to spend a week with my mother, and <u>she was explaining</u> why we had to bake the next day. It had to do with a play. A carpenter bakes his first loaf of bread. The other characters—his girlfriend, a social worker, two residents of a psychiatric hospital, and a neighborhood woman—eat it.

"Is that symbolic?" I said.

"I don't know about things like that, Ida," she said. Like the carpenter, she'd never baked bread before.[†]

Following is a sequence of three scenes:

<u>In a copy</u> of the Yale Calendar lying on a colleague's desk, Charlotte spotted a notice. Professor Luis Talamante, chair of the Chicano Studies Department at the California State University at Chico, was to lecture. For a moment she thought it had to be an older man with the same name as the boy she'd worked with in Fresno, but then she realized that Luis would now be forty-three. Of course it still might just be someone with the same name. His topic was "The Politics of Irrigation in the American Southwest." She made a note of the date and place. She tried to remember the silent boy she'd worked with.

---

[*] First the author makes a remark about how things "would be," that is, the *condition* of things. She actually enters the scene with Ida's remark, switching back to a sentence of orientation of how they came to be together.

[†] This is the beginning of a new story. We don't know yet if the narrator is male or female, but we find out on the next page (female). And we are pulled right into a setting (the kitchen) with the narrator's mother, engaged in an activity.

The old man's oldest son complained about Charlotte to the director of the clinic. He asked to have his father assigned to a different social worker. That hadn't happened to Charlotte before. <u>The director spoke</u> earnestly to her about it. "I made some mistakes," said Charlotte.

"He's a difficult person. But he said you were abusive."

"I doubt it."

Charlotte had just finished work for the day and she drove to Daisy's apartment. <u>Daisy was packing</u> pots and pans; she had found an apartment and signed a lease, and she was moving in just a few days. "Was I drunk that night?" said Charlotte.

"On one glass of wine?"*

Now let's look at two chapter openings from Tom Drury's *Hunts in Dreams,* a novel about an action-packed October weekend in the lives of a family in the Midwest.

In the opening chapter, "Charles," Charles goes to a gun shop. He wants the owners to buy a very special gun from a minister's widow and then turn around and sell it to him. It takes the scene for this to get spelled out. The scene begins as follows, going straight into the interaction among the characters. This excerpt is followed by dialogue.

The man behind the counter of the gun shop did not understand what Charles wanted, and so he summoned his sister from the back room, and she did not understand either. It was late on a Friday afternoon in October, and Charles seemed to be speaking an unknown language.

At the beginning of chapter 3, "Joan," Drury again begins with a scene, but this time he has his POV character reflect about the

---

* This passage is a little more complicated. It comes in the middle of a story, and it is an example of a very economical scene sequence. First we see Charlotte in her office looking at a flyer. (Later she goes to the lecture.) Then we switch to a summary of a tiny bit of background having to do with her job, going into a new scene, followed by yet another sentence of transition and a new scene. Study the passage for its economy and fluidity. The whole book is worth studying.

state of things before she opens her interaction with the man in charge of the gas station. The paragraph of musing isn't exactly related to the matter at hand, but it wonderfully reveals Joan's manner of thinking and prepares the reader for her behavior in the scene.

The man in charge of the gas station wore a green button that said

Jim
I Am Empowered
To Serve
You

This made Joan think, as she had more and more lately, that something was happening to the country. It no longer had the solid feel of any place she was used to. Just the other night a man called the house to say that Joan's family had been chosen from many potential applicants to receive a loan with which to pay down their debt. She pointed out that her family did not have any debt to speak of and that a loan, which was itself debt, could not be very accurately said to pay debt down. The caller replied that he was only reading what was put before him and that he did not wish to argue about the wording, which was not his.

"The pump won't work," she told Jim.

In her fine story collection *The Necessary Grace to Fall,* Gina Ochsner models numerous strategies for winding in and out of near and far history (summary) and scene. Let's look at some of her transitions into scenes in the story "What Holds Us Fast" as examples.

She opens the story with the sentence "From the time she was eight, when she suddenly lost her dog to a disease she'd never heard of but that sounded like a Mexican beet, Claire had been watching and waiting for death." At the end of that paragraph of reflection, she says, "But what people tended to forget, Claire realized one day as she emptied her grandmother's drainage shunt, was that the pain of dying and living were re-markably the same." In one paragraph, the theme of the story has been established beautifully, but the story itself unfolds in sur-prising ways.

The next paragraph begins with this scene fragment:

"When will the living not hurt so much?" Eugenia asked Claire as she leaned on her granddaughter and half walked, half crawled to the bathtub. [Opens in medias res: a quick image of Claire caring for her sick grandmother.]

Here are some of the transitions into scenes in the story:

One day Claire read to Eugenia from the newspaper that some high school kids had taken the statue of Ronald McDonald from a local McDonald's and held it for ransom. [Classic "one day" opening]

Claire turned to the obituaries and read aloud while Eugenia sat propped against her pillows, her address book open. [Estab-lishes the scene; we know where we are and what is going on.]

When Claire read the obituaries to her grandmother, she was struck with the sparse descriptions, impressed by the brevity with which each person could be dispatched in print. [Opens scene with a comment about something on the character's mind; the scene goes on between Claire and her boyfriend Ray: Claire asks him what he thinks of obituaries, then goes on to reveal what she thinks of him and their relationship.]

"What are you afraid of?" Ray asked one night. They had gone out for dinner and were walking across the gravel lot back to Ray's truck. [Again, a classic opening: a line of dialogue, and then the establishment of the where and what of the scene so we know what's going on]

"What was it like?" Jeannette asked later, after Claire had been
released and they were driving back to Claire's Chevette. [Note
the way this provides a transition that indicates time has passed
from the previous scene.]

From *Occasions of Sin, a Memoir.* The memoir is built of summary
and essay more than of scene, so the scenes are more integrated than
in a novel; they don't "stand alone" so much. They also appear in
short fragments to illustrate points in the flow of discussion. Occasionally, a short scene does appear, and the opening sentence has to
establish the context (time, place) in the flow of the narrator's childhood history. I've chosen a few of those as examples.

One Sunday Mother wasn't feeling well so she lay on my
grandmother's bed most of the afternoon, her face turned to the
inside wall toward a paper field of buttercups on cream browned
by age like something baking.

Outside Oklahoma City, half a day from home, the car broke
down. We stood around on the side of the road while Daddy
poked at things under the hood.

One day, putting away some laundry in Mother's room, I saw
a shoebox I knew was stuffed with photographs and I hauled it
out and put it on her bed.

In her classic novel of Mexico, *Stones for Ibarra,* Harriet Doerr
uses various strategies to open scenes and chapters. I've chosen
several that illustrate transitions from the larger narrative to the
particular scene. In each of the following examples, note the way
place and/or time is deftly established. I have underlined some of
the transition signal words.

<u>On the day of</u> the inauguration a tasseled silk Mexican flag
flew from the hoist tower of the Malagueña mine, and children in

the costumes of Jalisco and Veracruz danced on the drenched ground.

   And now, a year later, Sara waited for Richard in the becalmed dining room of the Hotel Paris, which was gradually filling with vineyard owners and salesmen traveling for IBM or Datsun.

   It was almost three when he came up behind her, reached over her shoulder, and spread all twenty sections of a lottery ticket across the napkin still folded on her plate.

   One summer day after a rainstorm Sara Everton walked up the road, under the washed leaves of the ash trees, past the row of weather-streaked cells, and into the chapel of Tepozán.

Choose a scene you have been working on. Write for it opening paragraphs that are modeled directly after scenes you like. See how they move into the beats of the scene. Try different strategies for the same scene and see what works best. Rewrite the modeled paragraphs to make them wholly your own.

I've also found that if you take an interesting opening and use it as a model to write your own, you often find yourself taking off into a story. Later, you can rewrite the opening so that it doesn't too closely mimic the model. Or just devote a day, or a week, to writing openings. You might surprise yourself and build quite an inventory.

Exercises

Choose a scene or scene summary you have already written or planned. Experiment with sentences that open directly on the action.
   a. Open on dialogue, and quickly establish who is speaking and what is going on.
   b. Open on a description of someone in the middle of an action.

   c. Open on a description of an element of a setting and then immediately introduce the character who belongs in that setting and in the scene.

Look for scenes that come out of summary narrative into the close-up of the scene, and try writing that kind of movement into the beats of the scene.

   a. Write a paragraph or two of summary about a period of time that was important to you in your childhood— a summer when you went to camp; the time your family moved; the fall you started middle school, etc. Write a transition into a scene that brings you into a specific day and a specific event. (See "Advanced scene exercise" on p. 154 for a more sophisticated version of this exercise.)

   b. Write a summary about a character's relationship with his/her spouse and then create a transition into the scene when they have a serious confrontation, a terrible revelation, an accident, or some other dramatic event that you would render in the scene. Write the transition sentences that move the narrative from the overview of the relationship to a particular time and place.

A word or two about scene endings

You can almost say ditto to the scene-opening strategies when thinking about how to close a scene. You want to get *out* of the scene as smoothly as you can, as early as you can, leaving the reader with the appropriate emotional attitude toward the character and the story for that point in the narrative.

- You can just stop.
- You can comment on some aspect of the scene's action or the characters.

- You can "pull back" to comment on the larger story, or on life itself.

In simplest terms, I ask myself:

> Do I want the scene's action and emotions to feel closed or open when the scene ends?

If the action and emotions feel closed, it means that the scene has moved the story to a place where something has happened that solved a problem or nudged the character to a new and relatively satisfactory place in the development of his or her goals. Or it means that the opportunity to solve the problems or to reach the goals is over, that there is no more hope, and that the future is like a door shut against the character. You can see that a *closed scene ending* can be happy or sad, optimistic or pessimistic. It can be, truly, the end, or it can be a setback.

A scene that ends in a way that feels *open,* on the other hand, leaves the reader with questions in mind. Perhaps a new plot point was raised, and now we wonder what will happen next. Perhaps new facets of the character were revealed and they must be played out in future action. The expectation is that there is more to come.

If the scene is truly the end of a story and it has an open ending, it means that it leaves us feeling that the character is walking into the future, that the story isn't really over just because the telling stops.

So your decision about how to end your scene should first answer that question: *Is this scene open or closed?*

You choose the action beat that resolves the tension in the scene event (remembering that tension can be resolved in several different ways). Depending on what that resolution is, you decide how to convey the last emotional beat of the scene.

Sometimes you want to cut the scene short, like a jump-cut in a movie. Sometimes you will feel the need for a passage in which the POV character or possibly the voice of the narrator responds to what has happened in the scene, putting it into some kind of perspective, perhaps speculating on its meaning or on the future of those affected by it.

Look to your reading for models; decide what strategies the writers are using; try them in your own writing.

Advanced scene exercise: Phase narrative

Using a memory of your own life or a memory in the life of one of your characters in a story, cover a period of time (a "phase," such as a summer, or a holiday season, or the first semester of college, etc.) in this exercise. Write a generous narrative summary telling *in general* what happened in that phase of the life of the character. Then make a transition to a particular portion of that period that has special significance. This will probably require you to continue the narrative summary for a short while. Feel free to use scene fragments to make the narrative vivid and specific.

Then enter into a scene that opens onto a turning point in the life of the character. Take your time, setting the stage for the scene. This first scene introduces the important part of the memory; it does not have to tell the important thing that happened. It might simply tell what happened that *led* to what happened, or that brought a new person into the picture, etc. It's the scene that goes from narrative to saying, "And *then*—"

The point of the exercise is to go from a large long view (the narrative summary) to opening onto the close view required for a scene. Think of the scene as the first in a scene sequence.

At the end of the scene, what question will you have raised, or what problem will have been established? What desire will have been heightened?

This might launch you into a story.

If you are working with a small group, begin by going around and having everyone talk about the phase he or she will be writing about. In the course of telling it aloud, you will hear the sweep of the narrative. Have the members of your group write down titles for the stories they hear emerging, almost like captions. This gives you a sense of what your readers might think your story is about, and may give you ideas about how you want to focus your text. When everyone has had a turn, tell each other the titles. Don't get caught up in discussion of the stories. Just go write.

Later, you can talk about what you learned in telling the story, what you learned from the feedback in the titles, and what you learned from writing the scene itself. I have found, over and over again, that writers discover elements of their stories they were blind to before the group work.

11

BIG SCENES

SCENES THAT HAVE MANY CHARACTERS

- WHAT ARE SOME PLANNING STRATEGIES FOR SCENES WITH MANY CHARACTERS?
- EXERCISES

Some of us are planners, and some of us like to jump right in. Either way, we can find ourselves shaking with trepidation when facing a challenging writing task. Gustave Flaubert, writing *Madame Bovary,* conveyed to his friends over and over again the terror he felt as he came upon each new difficulty. Embarking on writing the scene at the inn on the evening of the Bovarys' arrival in their new town, he wrote in a letter, "Never in my life have I written anything more difficult than what I am doing now—trivial dialogue. I have to portray, simultaneously and in the same conversation, five or six characters who speak, several others who are spoken about, the scene, and the whole town, giving physical descriptions of people and objects; and in the midst of all that I have to show a man and a woman who are beginning . . . to fall in love with each other . . ."

Let me point out, straight away, that Flaubert had a detailed synopsis of his plot worked out before he started writing the book. There were many things still to discover and invent, and many changes, but he had a place to start.

I can't imagine writing a big scene without spending time preparing, though I'm sure there are writers of different temperament who wade in, flail about, and finally make their way just fine. And now that I think about it, by the time I am "preparing," I have been thinking and scribbling and making false starts for a long time. I've probably walked through versions of the scene in my mind many times, rejected them, absorbed bits and pieces, and only then think of myself as beginning.

Sometimes writing is exploring in the dark, the gathering of evidence of a story yet unseen, the story that is in you where you can't yet touch it. There are instances when you fly blind and trust your characters to tell you what they want to do. It happens, believe it or not, but you have to have a lot of patience with ambiguity. So, when I'm asked, "How do you write a big scene, with lots of characters? How do you manage all that is going on?" my answer is that you approach it much as you would the preparation of a huge Christmas dinner, a school play, or any other event that has many components. You think about who is there, what they are doing, and what the outcome is supposed to be. Remember: **situation/ action line/new situation.** As you proceed, you may find that it is convenient to think of the big scene as having a beginning (set up the situation), middle (line of action), and end (move to a new situation); and each of those parts as having its own little arc (progression from beginning to end, through events that result in some sort of outcome). And you definitely think of yourself as *drafting* the scene: You will probably start too early, go too fast, or else cram in too much; or stop too early or continue too late. But you must begin.

In the case of a fictional scene or chapter, the overall arc is probably going to be something dramatic. One of the things you can think about early—perhaps arbitrarily, in order to get started—is where the *high action, focal point,* or *most dramatic point* of the scene is. It makes a difference whether you are building toward a climax or recovering from an explosion. And you can always decide to do it another way. Drafts are not rationed!

I suggest that you begin by considering this:

Action and place are looked at from outside in,
but emotion is built from inside out.

In other words, there has to be an *event* (a familiar chorus, by now?), and it has to take place in a *setting*. So think those things through thoroughly: where you are, what is going on. Think like a movie director or perhaps an art director on a film, pulling back to see the way it all looks. Let your awareness of the *scene pulse* guide you in planning action. I find it helpful to sketch out a loose floor plan and to list the main *beats of action*.

Event has two closely allied meanings in the big scene. You are of course familiar with the one that refers to the overall action of the scene "adding up" to something meaningful. In the big scene, though, we have to consider a second meaning—a reason for the characters to be together. *Occasion* is a good word for this meaning of event. Big scenes arise out of weddings, funerals, holiday celebrations, parties, street fights, and so on. More interestingly, they arise out of occasions that are less familiar, even accidental reasons to pull people together. Last fall when, in my city's park, one dog attacked another dog and killed it, then turned on the owner, a convocation of people gathered around them. Fortunately, they were able to thwart the attack, but you can imagine the drama that ensued—the dead dog's owner's grief, anger, fear, pain; the attacking dog's owner's defensiveness, sorrow, chagrin, etc. This real-life scene has had continuing reverberations in my dog-loving, leash-hating community.

Obviously, a big scene has to be about something meaningful. A huge parade could actually be a static scene. What's the point? You'll find it helpful to go back to the basics:

- What's the tension here, and what becomes of it?
- What are the beats of action? How do they link in pairs of action-reaction?
- *Focus carefully on your POV character.* In a sense, that focus is your life jacket as you jump into deep water.

Ask yourself:
- What is the occasion for these people to be together?

• Where are these people (especially my POV character) emotionally, and in terms of power, at the beginning of the big scene?

• Where are they at the end? In other words, what has changed? Consider in particular the shift in circumstances and emotions of your POV character. This is what I mean by coming in close: emotion writ small. You are working from within one character, watching the scene from there, letting emotions spill in concentric circles from that character:

   a. From nervousness to elation
   b. From giddy comradeship to angry dismissal
   c. From hope to sorrow
   d. From desire to despair

And so on. Each of these phrases represents the way the POV character stands in relation to others in the scene, or perhaps to one significant other.

Get a handle on this shift, and you'll know that you have to get from that first "constellation" to the end one. Everything coalesces around that core emotional journey *played out in beats of action*.

I spend days on such scenes. I daydream. I take long walks. I talk to myself. I sketch out bits of dialogue. Sometimes I lie on the couch in a fugue state and my husband, coming upon me, asks, "Are you okay? Is there something I can get you?"

Then I start to develop a kind of *scenario* or *summary:*

• What time of day is it, and how does that affect the light, the feel of the space?

• Is everyone on hand, or are there arrivals and departures?

• What topics are discussed, argued, or avoided?

• How can I keep the focus where I want it? Will the POV character be commenting on what is going on throughout, or mostly at the end? It might be a good first round to write the scene as all action and dialogue, then do it over again, integrating the interior responses. Or write a simple dramatic summary before fleshing out the scene. Try it different ways to see what works for you.

• What are my key moments, and how do they stand out from the general action?

• What is the pulse? Is there a building of tension and pace?

You see, a big scene is really like a story:
  • It has to have a beginning, middle, and end;
  • It has a setting;
  • It has a pulse;
  • It builds;
  • It ends with something changed or shifted.

Don't worry too much about where you start; in revision, you can tighten the scene, maybe entering later. For now, begin where you feel most confident and enthusiastic.

Include what seems relevant, what makes the scene vibrate with life. The things going on in the background provide both a *projection* of what is going on in the central tension and a *contrast* to it.

Don't worry if this makes your head swim. It's not the easiest work. There's plenty to learn as you advance, but for now, simply work like an apprentice, one foot in front of the other, one brick then the mortar. It's the work of the artisan, part day labor and part inspiration. It gets better the longer you work at it.

I can't say how another writer plans such work, so I am going to use a scene from one of my own novels. Then I will mention a scene from another writer, speaking not of the writer but of the *reading-writer* who is trying to learn from models.

The small-focus big scene

Early in *A Chance to See Egypt,* the narration tells a little about Riley's first encounter with Eva, his dead wife. Although this scene has a lot of characters and things going on, it actually has a very small focus: Riley and Eva. So it is an example of an easy way to manage the big scene. Keep it in mind, because you will find sometimes that the scene you think of as so big is really a small scene inside a big setting, like this one.

Here is what I thought about before I started:

1. *Function* (Why have this scene?): I wanted this to be the scene where Riley meets Eva. This is a *plot point*. It is also a scene that reveals a part of Riley's nature: his pleasure in small talk with people. This is a *character point*. Many scenes are written to reveal character, but they do it best if they move the story along, too.

2. *Setting and major event:* The christening of Riley's neighbor's twin granddaughters. I got the whole idea at lunch one day, when such a party took place at the opposite end of the restaurant patio where I was eating.

3. *Characters:* I made a list of who would be there, and who might interact with Riley. This changed a little as I wrote, but I already had a good grasp of the grandmother character, for example. I made notes of little character quirks that could emerge.

4. *Activity:* Other than the "main event," meeting Eva, and the fact that it is a christening, I wanted certain beats: toasts, Riley engaged with some of the relatives (which prefigures his easy engagement with people in the Mexican village), and dancing. Things have to be going on! Sometimes you will write such a scene and discover in revision that a few subtle additions or changes will make the scene shimmer with the future, even though the reader won't recognize it until later.

5. *Pulse:* The energy and happiness of the celebration; Riley's openheartedness.'

6. *Focal point:* Riley makes his way to Eva.

Basically, this is a scene in which Riley finds himself at home with another family, and then, out of nowhere, he is blindsided by Eva.

He met Eva at the christening of his neighbor Oscar Munoz's twin granddaughters, children of a daughter. The party clustered on the church steps for photographs. Felipa Munoz introduced them. They all trooped down the walk and across the street onto a shady sidewalk. The restaurant was three blocks away. Drivers of cars going by honked at them. They made a merry parade, the young parents leading the way with the babies' long white dresses trailing to their knees. The grandmothers carried armloads of flowers.

"I took Mrs. Iruegas and her mother to Fatima last year," Eva said.

"You are a godparent too?"

"And a travel agent," she said. "Avalon Tours, over on Belden. Here, take my card."

The restaurant had arranged long tables in a U shape and hung awnings to shade them from the midday sun. On the tables were photographs in silver frames—pictures of the couple on their wedding day, and studio portraits of the babies in their christening dresses. At each plate was a wallet-sized picture of the babies. Riley tucked his into a pocket. They had champagne in fluted glasses, and toasted the children and their parents.

Riley had consulted his Spanish teacher. He said, "To the great joy of tender babies," and everyone clapped.

Eva Wasierski said, "To family, community, and love," and they murmured approval. She had seated herself next to Mrs. Iruegas, with one of the young relatives on the other side.

Riley sat at the other table across the U from her. The waiters brought out a lavish lunch on white platters. Oscar's son wanted Riley's advice about dogs; his boys were begging for a puppy. Riley suggested they look at the pound first. Before he knew what had happened, he had agreed to go along. He realized suddenly that as godfather to these children, he would be part of the extended family, asked for advice and favors and companionship through the years. It pleased him to think it.

Mrs. Iruegas's old mother—everyone, relative or not, called her Abuela—put her cool dry hand on Riley's and leaned close to speak in a gravelly whisper. "The twins come from my side of the family." She spoke in Spanish, but with such precise enunciation, Riley understood quite well. She said, "My sister and I were identical. She died in a great flu epidemic along with Mama. Then my first baby was kicked in the head by a horse. The rider did not even stop to see what he had done."

"Life is hard," Riley said.

The old woman shook her finger in the direction of the babies. Their mother had removed the gowns and they lay in their car seats on the tabletop, dressed in pink shirts and diapers, their feet wiggling in the warm air. "We never mix them up," Abuela said.

At first Riley did not understand. "The babies?" he asked.

The old woman cackled. She pointed to the pink-shirted twins. "Girl babies," she said. Then she wagged her finger toward Oscar, who had one of his twin grandsons on his lap, the child of his son. "Boy babies."

The band came in and began to play. People from inside the restaurant stood in the wide doorway or stepped off onto the court paving to watch. The babies' mother took one of the infants against her, and her mother helped her drape a fine cotton shawl elaborately over her shoulder and the child so that her breast was not exposed by nursing. Half a dozen little children ran around wildly, inspired, no doubt, by the riotous tunes from the musicians, who wore starched shirts and broad scarlet cummerbunds. The babies' father took his own mother to the center of the courtyard, where the paving stones were smoothest. She was laughing and shaking her head. Oscar went over to the musicians and spoke to them. They began playing a sweet melodic song. Oscar helped his wife up from her chair to dance.

Riley made his way to Eva Wasierski. There was something almost formidable about her—her wide eyes, her carefully arranged brown hair. She had the look of someone used to authority, like a school principal.

The chair next to her was empty now, and at the last moment his courage left him and he sat down instead of asking her to dance. He said, "It's a nice party, isn't it?"

She smiled and nodded. She was watching the dancing couples. One fat uncle was mopping his forehead with a large handkerchief.

"Have you known them long?" Riley asked.

"They are all frequent flyers," she said. "I have sent these ladies to Guadalajara many times."

"I've never been."

"To Mexico?"

"Anywhere," he blurted, then regretted it. She would know him for the boring man he was.

"You've missed the summer sales." She was giving him her full attention now. "But fall is the best time to travel anyway."

"I don't have any plans—"

"Planning is my vocation. Now, do you dance, Mr. Riley?"

I included this entire passage because although it covers a reasonably long period of time, it is not a very long passage. You will note that much of what is going on is summarized, such as the discussion about getting a dog. We are "there" in the sense that we feel present at the party, but we don't hear all the dialogue and take up so much space in the story. That longer space—coming in close, as a scene does—is saved for Riley's interactions with the old grandmother (showing his ease with her) and with Eva (showing his awkwardness and her authority).

Note, also, that the scene begins with a movement, a small journey, if you will, as the christening party leaves the church and makes its way to the restaurant. Then the scene ends with the launching of a new journey—Riley's relationship with Eva, which is itself begun by a discussion of travel.

What changes in this scene is that Mr. Riley, good guy and neighbor, who does so well with people in general, finds himself engaged with one particular woman. He is the focus of the entire scene.

There are other "big scenes" late in this book: a fiesta and a wedding. Basically, I planned them like plays. I listed my characters and planned when I would "bring people on." I also tried to exploit the setting—the people in the background, and so on. But because two people were at the heart of each chapter, it turned out not to be so difficult after all. List the beats, write the scene.

Big scenes with multiple foci

Robert Boswell writes a messy scene sequence near the end of his terrific novel *Mystery Ride,* with a big cast of minor characters surrounding a family that breaks up and reinvents itself. You just need to know that Dulcie is the teenage daughter of Angela and Stephen, who at this point have parted. Angela, now with Quin, is hugely pregnant. She wanted Dulcie to come see her in California from the midwestern farm where Dulcie lives with her father, and when Dulcie refused, Stephen suggested that they all meet in Tucson at the house of Stephen's brother, Andrew. Stephen's girlfriend, Gabriela, also appears.

First everyone arrives in time for dinner. At the point we are entering this building scene sequence, mother and daughter are at it. The shape of the scene is fascinating. Watch how the tension between the daughter and mother escalates while others present try to defuse the situation, until, in fact, Quin is able to do so with a little story he tells.

At this point, the tension has lessened greatly. Everyone comes to the table—a new scene, marked by "They all came to the table then, the animosity, for the moment, discharged"—and they begin discussing names for Angela's baby. Out of nowhere (really?) Dulcie is finally able to say what's really on her mind to her mother. The whole tone between them is different by then.

So the tension that already exists comes roaring out as soon as people are gathered; someone defuses it; gentle, peripheral conversation helps maintain the peace; and Dulcie finally feels safe to say what's on her mind and give her mother a chance to respond. It's a beautifully orchestrated scene, with the "big hump" of conflict about two-thirds of the way through.

You can think of the passage, starting "They gathered for Christmas Eve at the adobe house on Water Street" and ending "And so the meal continued, peacefully," as having these parts:

1. Arrival scene: This orients the reader to the house and brings the characters onstage. It has three small sections: Angela and Quin come; Stephen and Dulcie come; Gabriela comes.

2. Quarrel: In the kitchen, Dulcie and Angela quarrel about Dulcie's clothes. Various others try to intervene, until Quin tells a story and provides a transition to dinner.

3. Dinner: They discuss the coming baby, there's a trailing off of the conversation, and then Dulcie pulls it back to her mother.

An argument was going on in the kitchen. Dulcie had torn open the boxes of clothes and complained that her mother had left her best things in California. "I'm not going to move back just to get my stuff," she said.

"Everything you asked for is in those boxes," Angela said flatly.

"Gabbie," Andrew said happily. "You made it."

Gabriela waved to him from the door. "Where should we put your brother's luggage?" she asked.

Andrew rushed over to grab the bag she carried. He introduced her. "I didn't tell you she was coming," he said, looking at Angela, "because I was afraid she wouldn't make it, and then you'd all think I was a liar."

"Where's my green sweater?" Dulcie demanded.

"Can't this wait?" Angela asked her.

Dulcie shoved the box across the tile floor. "Of course, it just *happens* to be the sweater you always borrow from me that you forgot to bring."

Stephen said, "You have a green sweater at the farm."

"It's not the same sweater," Dulcie insisted. "I should have known you'd be on her side. No matter what she does to you, you always stand up for her. You're pathetic."

"I may well be, but you do have a green sweater in Iowa," he said.

"Maybe we should eat," Andrew said. To Gabbie, he added, "I made the turkey."

"Brave soul," she said. "I was sure you'd chicken out—so to speak."

"Great, a comedian," Dulcie said. "A knocked-up thief, a comedian, and a pathetic manure head all at the same table."

"I want you to apologize immediately," Angela said, angry now.

"Why should I care what you want?" Dulcie responded and sat on the floor, planting her elbows on one of her boxes.

"Is this the way you let her act?" Angela demanded of Stephen.

Quin, who had been removing plastic wrap from a dozen side dishes Andrew had prepared, suddenly spoke in a loud and clear voice, to no one in particular. "Have you ever noticed," he began, "how the odor of tuna, if not covered properly, will spread in a refrigerator and color the taste of everything? Even chocolate mousse will taste of tuna?"

It was such an odd question and asked with such a loud and demanding tone that no one knew how to answer.

"Tuna with turkey?" Gabbie asked Andrew, but he shook his head.

Quin continued, evidently expecting no response. "One sour apple doesn't spoil the whole bunch, but it may spoil your taste for apples."

"What are you getting at, Quin?" asked Stephen.

"Leave him alone," Dulcie said angrily.

"My father and I used to squabble," Quin went on, unflustered. "There was one summer day when I was fifteen and working at a bowling alley, when my father had come to tell me something or other, and found me in the back room with my shirt open and flapping my arms. I was imitating one of the customers for the entertainment of the other boys who worked there. He didn't say anything to me, but what a look he gave me, what a look. When he got me to the car he said, 'Is that the way you behave when I'm not around?'" Quin paused and put his hands in his pockets. He had been folding the strips of clear plastic wrap into little squares, which he now placed on the counter. He leaned over the turkey, so that his cheek was near enough to feel the radiating heat. He lifted his head and smiled. "I think it's ready to be carved," he said.

They all came to the table then, the animosity, for the moment, discharged.

[And then, after the desultory talk I described above—]

"You know what it is," Dulcie said suddenly to her mother, and the discussion of Central America stopped. "I've got this idea that you don't really have feelings. Not real ones. How do you suppose I got that into my head?"

Angela spoke softly. "I don't know." Then she added, "I've missed you. I really have."

"Yeah," Dulcie said. "It amazes me, too."

And so the meal continued, peacefully.

See how the line of Dulcie/Angela cuts right through everything else that is going on? I could easily have included this same passage in chapter 7, "Negotiation." It illustrates first how high tension is defused; and then, at the end, how it is resolved. It's a lovely progression.

In this passage, one character provides the focus of the scene, teen daughter Dulcie. The sharp focus helps you to construct the scene because you know what you have to keep coming back to, and where the string of tension is being pulled.

Tackle your own big scene. Dream your dream, make your lists, roll up your sleeves, and get at it. Give yourself a lot of slack and a lot of time.

Exercises

• *Small Focus, Big Scene:* Plan a scene in which the focus is on the interaction of two people within the context of a larger gathering. Perhaps they bring a conflict into the scene, or something about the scene causes one of them to raise an issue. (Two different strategies!) Put them into a situation with other people where they are unable to work out a sustained amount of time without interruption, and so the tension between them intensifies but is not resolved. Remember that one of them will be your POV character; have that character interact with others, too.

Try planning the scene first, following the format I described above, sketching out the *setting, characters, and event.* You may want to list some of the *beats,* too.

Establish the scene with lots of visual information, so that the reader sees what is going on around your key characters. It is helpful if you have made a list of objects in the room and other elements of the setting that may be used or appear or be referred to in the scene.

• *Reading Big Scenes for Beats:* Read a big scene several times until you feel you have the flow of it and can hold it in your mind. Then study its elements. Identify the focus in the scene: What does it keep coming back to? A topic of conversation or disagreement? A person? An event in the past or one that is about to happen? Take the scene apart by listing the beats of action. Now go over those beats and star or underline those that are the most important, those that form the heart of the scene, *that are related to the focal issue or person.* What, then, is the effect of the other beats? Do they simply make it possible for the core actions to happen, or do they amplify them in some way? Identify the point where there is either confrontation or a clear avoidance of it that ends with unresolved conflict that will carry over into another scene.

Consider how the nature of the event itself and the environment contribute to the flow of beats and the movement of the dramatic action.

This is a lot of work! You might begin by looking at a scene and concentrating on only one element of analysis, then coming back and adding another, or possibly moving on to another scene and considering two elements this time, and so on.

The best examples will be those you have enjoyed and admired. All in all, big scenes are challenging. If you feel put off, that's fine. Maybe you'll think like the creative writing instructor in Alice Munro's story "Differently" who tells a character about her writing: "Too many things. Too many things going on at the same time; also too many people. Think, he told her. What is the important thing? What do you want us to pay attention to? Think."

• *Big Scene Dossier:* Spend some time imagining circumstances and characters that might combine in a suitable setting to make a big scene. List as many kinds of settings, circumstances, and occasions as you can think of where people could gather.

Select one at a time and think of a conflict that might arise out of the event or situation itself (such as a fight in a bar). Then think of a conflict that might arise in such a situation that would have nothing to do with the situation or event itself, but could get played out there. (Family and friends confronting a "user" at a birthday party where he is spoiling the fun. Or an unexpected pregnancy being revealed at a business conference. And so on.)

The idea is simply to stretch your mind around the possibilities. Keep adding to your list.

Here are some suggested models:

a. Eudora Welty's *Losing Battles*. Three generations of Granny Vaughn's relatives gather for her ninetieth birthday. The novel is built of dialogue and more dialogue, along with small actions and descriptions. There are many scenes that would serve as models.

b. V. S. Naipaul's *Half a Life*. There is a quiet scene in this story of a man whose father married a woman of low caste. The scene is a gathering of literary types, an editor and some writers. There is a good deal of cross talk, but the action is minimal, although it does keep us aware of the setting. It is a fine scene to allay your fears—it doesn't seem formidable—at the same time that you can read it again and again to learn how Naipaul creates meaning with subtlety and grace and great sophistication.

c. Haruki Murakami's "Lieutenant Mamiya's Long Story: Part II" from *The Wind-Up Bird Chronicle* (also excerpted in *Vintage Murakami*). You can't really call this a crowd scene, but there are several characters, and it's worth looking at how the author handles the movement of focus from one to another. The narrator tells about being captured by two Mongolian soldiers during World War II. The narrator is one of four soldiers. So you have six men in this section of the story, but it is never the least bit "crowded."

d. Charles Baxter's story "Reincarnation." The story is about the last hours of a summer dinner party in which three couples discuss their earlier lives and those moments that had special power, and indeed still do. It's a wonderful story, and a masterful job of handling what is essentially a static situation: six people talking! Study how, in fact, he keeps the reader in the scene, aware of these characters and their surroundings, their movements, and their emotions. Things do "happen" here.

PART FOUR

MOVING TO INDEPENDENT STUDY

12

READING FOR STORY AND SCENE

LEARNING TO READ SCENES AS A WRITER

READ TO DEEPEN YOUR KNOWLEDGE OF SCENE STRATEGIES.

■ REVIEW KEY VOCABULARY FOR TALKING ABOUT SCENES
■ REVIEW QUESTIONS TO GUIDE YOUR ANALYSIS OF SCENES
■ CONSIDER QUESTIONS ABOUT WHOLE STORIES, TO PUT SCENES IN CONTEXT

Review vocabulary

You have become familiar by now with the idea of *event* and *emotion* in the scene, and the ways that these are built through *beats* of action.

You are conscious of the ways that scenes contribute to the development of a story, fulfilling *functions* in the story, such as revealing character, giving necessary information, introducing plot turns, and so on.

You know that every scene has a *pulse* that is like the heartbeat beneath the action; another way of thinking of this is to consider the source of the scene's *tension*.

The scene is shaped artfully, and we call that shape its *structure*. You can present a scene whole, like a little story. You can use a partial scene, presented elliptically. Or fragments—little pieces of it that hint at the whole—can be set into longer passages of narrative summary, or stand more or less alone as a tiny block within the narrative.

If you are more comfortable calling my "elements" or concepts by other names, by all means write your terms in beside mine. Likewise, as you read other craft books, attend workshops and classes, and so on, amend these descriptions in whatever way makes sense to you. The goal is for you to become your own teacher through your reading and self-evaluation.

On the pages that follow, I present three different models to guide an analysis of a scene from a story or novel. You would not use all with each scene, or in one sitting. Rather, you will find the first to be easiest, the second to be slightly more analytical. The third model focuses not on the scene as it stands alone but on its place in the whole story.

There are scenes in the next sections that can be used for practice, but ultimately you will want to collect many samples of your own from writers you admire. The work of examining these passages closely will help you integrate the concepts you have been learning into your writing. Over time, you will tackle more complex models, and perhaps more complex writing, too.

First model: Review elements of the scene

This helps you to see how the scene is held together by important elements. It will become second nature for you to check for these elements in your writing.

Scene Elements
- *Event:* The core actions of the scene: what holds the scene together. What is the event in this scene? How do the actions add up to an overall effect?
- *Emotion:* The meaning of the action for characters in the scene; the feelings conveyed by the scene's actions. How do the characters (especially the POV character) react to the ac-

tions in the scene? What emotions are expressed? How does the reader feel at the end of the scene?

- *Pulse:* The underlying source of the scene's anxiety or excitement: a thread that is pulled through the scene by the action. What keeps the reader focused in this scene? What seems to compel the line of action?
- *Point-of-view character:* Which character's awareness guides the reader's awareness? Does the author take the reader inside the POV character's consciousness?
- *Structure:* How is the scene shaped? Is there a beginning, middle, and end? If not, can you imagine the "ghost" of what is missing? Why do you think the author used the scene elliptically (a part of it rather than whole)? What is the effect?

Second model: Scene analysis

1. Summarize the scene event. List the main beats of action. Can you pinpoint the focal point, where the beats seem to turn the action in a different direction?

2. Describe the emotional shift that takes place in the scene. Which character is the *center of consciousness*? Does this character control the power? Is there some kind of emotional negotiation or exchange? Is a tacit contract among characters broken, strengthened, or renegotiated?

3. What does the scene accomplish for the story? In what ways is it necessary?

4. How is the scene shaped? If it is not all in place (with a beginning, middle, and end), how are you oriented to the missing elements and the larger context of meaning?

5. What element of craft in this scene would you like to try out in your own writing?

Third model: Reading scenes in context

Here are some suggestions for reading scenes as they are set in the longer narrative. You can work with short stories or with novels or creative nonfiction, as long as you are able to select passages that "stand alone" enough for your analysis. Eventually you will start to see how writers thread narrative with scenic elements, sometimes with great subtlety and sophistication, but for now, if it's difficult to identify the shape of the scene, go to something easier.

Enjoy your reading. Make a deliberate effort to find new voices, to expand your very sense of voice and story. Work with passages that you love enough to read over and over again.

1. *How does the writer enter the story or scene?* If you think of a story as being part of a long line of events, and the opening of the story as cutting into that line somewhere, think of why the author started at this place. Does the story's history emerge in the present time of the story?

2. Try to think like this author: *What is a perfect story?* What does this story do and how does it do it? What do you especially like about this story? Can you see places where the author might have made a different choice, to different effect?

3. *What creates the story's pulse?* What element seems most important in creating the pull through the story, and its combustion? What makes the story feel urgent, i.e., worth telling? Look for specific moments that develop that urgency.

4. *How does the author handle dialogue?* Watch for how the speech of different characters differs. Consider the balance of direct discourse (in quotation marks) and indirect discourse

(things said but summarized). How are you alerted to who is speaking? How are beats of activity used to emphasize dialogue, provide rest, or increase tension?

5. *How is character developed?* What elements of action do this? Where is description used? Where are thoughts of characters used to reveal aspects of personality and emotion?

6. *Can you summarize the plot?* You will find that the more complex the story, the harder it is to say what happens without getting tangled up in your words. Step back and think about what happens in a macrosense: How are things different at the end?

At some point you will find it helpful to apply these same questions to your own stories. The answers will help you determine if you have done what you set out to do, and where you'll want to do more work.

13

EVALUATION

USING VARIOUS TEMPLATES TO EVALUATE YOUR OWN WRITING

USEFUL CRITERIA FOR EVALUATING A SCENE

- REVIEW THE BASIC ELEMENTS OF SCENE STRUCTURE
- ASSESS THE SCENE'S UTILITY AND ECONOMY
- EXPERIENCE THE SCENE FROM THE POINT OF VIEW OF THE MAIN CHARACTER
- IDENTIFY PROBLEMS

When you examine the draft of a scene you have written and know that it isn't what you hoped it would be, don't simply throw up your hands. And don't think that you can start with the first sentence and a colored pen, working your way through the text, fixing problems. You should think about the scene as a whole before you tackle it at the line level, as you are more likely to rewrite than to change a few words.

The basic strategy is to ask questions of yourself and of your work, and to do this over and over, so that your writing becomes clearer to you, and gets closer to what you intended for it to become. When I say that, I mean both in regard to a single piece of work—at different stages—and in regard to your body of work over time. Once you learn fundamental strategies, you will have natural impulses about the "basics" in your first drafts. At first, getting those things right may be your main effort. Later, though, you'll move on to innovation, when you are able to tolerate the rocky feeling of uneven new ground because you have learned how to talk to yourself about your writing.

Caveat I

Don't try to use all these criteria at one time for one scene. Start with a few questions. Add to them gradually. Eventually you'll learn to recognize problem areas and you won't be covering so many concepts for each scene.

Caveat II

When you are focusing on writing the scene, focus on making it the best you can, almost as if it were a story. Ultimately, however, you have to stand back and ask yourself how it fits into the larger story. That may mean dropping elements, or playing down introspection, action, description, or other elements. It may even mean dropping the scene entirely, reducing it to a mere summary, and you probably can't know that for sure until you have a draft of the story done.

Start by answering these fundamental questions:

- What is the *event* in the scene, and what emotions are connected to it? (Does the event merit a scene or could you just summarize it? Have you exploited it dramatically?)
- What did you want the scene to accomplish for the story, and does it accomplish this goal? (Caption the *function* of the scene with a word like one of these: Information, Confrontation, Decision, Revelation, Recognition, Catalyst, Reflection, Turning Point, Capitulation, Resolution.)
- Is it clear where the scene begins and ends? Is this the best place and *shape* for it?
- What is the *pulse* of the scene, and is it sufficient to drive the action and the feeling? Does the pulse accelerate through the scene and build to something?

These questions, which take you back to the beginning of the book, are the fundamentals of scene-building, and they may be a sufficient guide for you in revising for a while. If you belong to a writing group, these questions can provide a guide to your critiques.

Analyze the scene's utility and economy

You will probably write more scenes than you need, but you have to stand back, take a hard look, and figure out what counts. Before you do the work of revising, be sure this is a scene you need in your narrative. Why did you write it? Why did you place it there? What purpose does it serve in the larger story?

Sometimes you will realize that you wrote a scene in order to explore what is going on with a character; you had to walk through some action with close attention in order to understand motivation, or to make a decision about the next step in the plot. You may discover, however, that what you wrote can be reduced to a sentence or two of transition, if that. You may realize that you've been rewriting a set of circumstances or aspects of a relationship that you were working out in other scenes, and that what this exercise accomplished was to give you greater insight, so that you can go back and revise the earlier scene, or combine them, or perhaps eliminate the earlier one and revise this one.

Captioning the scene—giving it an expanded title that captures the essence of the event—is useful because it allows you to see if you have the same thing happening more than once and how scenes relate.

Ask yourself these questions:

- Do I have a clear purpose for this scene, and does the scene satisfy it? Answer by stating the purpose in a sentence and summarizing the key outcome(s) of the scene.
- Are there passages of flashback, description, or interior response that break up the flow of the scene too much? Can they be reduced or eliminated?

- Would it be possible to enter the scene at a later point?
- Would it be a loss if this scene were summarized or integrated into another scene? Be sure you are not unnecessarily repeating actions and character behaviors you have already
  explored. You want, always, to be adding something new to
  what has come before, illuminating aspects of character and
  pushing the plot forward.
- Is this the right place for the scene? Look at its place in the
  sequence of action surrounding it. It should arise out of
  what has come before and lead to what comes next.

Next, look at the scene in terms of the POV character

- Who is this character, and what does he or she want? How
  much does the desire matter to the character? To the scene?
  Is the pulse of the scene strongly related to this desire?
- What is his or her response to the event(s) of the scene? Is
  the response all interior, or can we also see it in the actions
  taken by the character?
- If you are going to pull the reader into this scene, we have
  to have someone to care about. In a sense, we have to share
  the character's fate. *Do we?*

Identify the scene's problems

Does your scene have any of these problems? All of them can be
"fixed" if the scene is basically strong. These concepts are all discussed in the book, so if you see a problem—tackle one at a
time!—review the principles governing a particular skill, and approach the scene revision optimistically.

- No clear event
    State the event you intended until you are satisfied that it
    is dramatic, significant, and large enough for a scene.

- No clear beats of action

  List those you can. Determine your intentions and write those beats. Now rewrite.

- No clear viewpoint

  Stick to one character's thoughts and feelings! When you are describing what other characters are doing, don't say what they are thinking; don't express their opinions except in dialogue. Let their behaviors speak for them. Then be sure you find ways to show your character reacting to actions and responding emotionally.

- No clear goal/intention for the characters

  So state one! Then see what you have to do to reshape the scene toward that goal. Is the goal thwarted or satisfied?

- Or, conversely, overly direct statement of purpose; no subtext or subtlety

  Don't give everything away too soon. Build a question into the first part of your scene, which the scene answers. If it doesn't, have you built suspense or muddiness?

- Overwritten description and activity

  For every line of description, ask yourself: How does this help the scene? What would happen if I took it out? Is it a cliché?

- Or insufficient grounding

  See your characters in place and time. Integrate lines of description into the action so that the reader sees them, too.

- Problems in dialogue: banality; no difference between the voices of the characters; goes on too long; too direct

  Write your dialogue on a new page, as if it is a play. No action or description. Just talk. How do you differentiate your characters? How do you develop them? Do they have certain habits of speech? Do they differ intellectually? Is one personality more volatile than another? Knowing your characters well will help you create apt dialogue. Then you can integrate it into the scene again.

- Lacks focal point

    Put a line down the middle of a page. On the left, list your beats of action. On the right, list the beats of emotion—moments of response. Look for ways to make these happen close to one another in a causally linked way. Make them accelerate in intensity and meaning. Find a place where the action can turn. Make sure your beats lead *up to* and then *away from* that point.

- Doesn't "add up"

    We're not left in a different place from where we started. If this is true, you have to rethink the scene entirely. What is the scene supposed to be about? What should it mean for the characters, and for the story? Does the scene lack conflict, pulse, event?

Which criteria seem most helpful to you? Make a short list for yourself and use that instead of the whole chapter for a while.

On the following pages there is a summary sheet of all the evaluation criteria, easy to copy for your regular use.

- Review the basic elements of scene structure
- Assess the scene's utility and economy
- Experience the scene from the point of view of the main character
- Identify problems

■ Start by answering these fundamental questions:

What is the **event** in the scene, and what emotions are connected to it? (Does the event merit a scene, or could you just summarize it? Have you exploited it dramatically?)

What did you want the scene to accomplish for the story, and does it accomplish this goal? (Caption the **function** of the scene with a word like one of these: Information, Confrontation, Decision, Revelation, Recognition, Catalyst, Reflection, Turning Point, Capitulation, Resolution.)

Is it clear where the scene begins and ends? Is this the best place and **shape** for it?

What is the **pulse** of the scene, and is it sufficient to drive the action and the feeling? Does the pulse accelerate through the scene and build to something?

■ Analyze the scene's utility and economy

You will probably write more scenes than you need, but you have to stand back, take a hard look, and figure out what counts. Before you do the work of revising, be sure this is a scene you need in your narrative. Why did you write it? Why did you place it there? What purpose does it serve in the larger story?

Captioning the scene—giving it an expanded title that captures the essence of the event—is useful because it allows you to see if you have the same thing happening more than once and how scenes relate.

■ Ask yourself these questions:

Do I have a clear purpose for this scene, and does the scene satisfy it? Answer by stating the purpose in a sentence and summarizing the key outcome(s) of the scene.

Are there passages of flashback, description, or interior response that break up the flow of the scene too much? Can they be reduced or eliminated?

Would it be possible to enter the scene at a later point?

Would it be a loss if this scene were summarized or integrated into another scene? Be sure you are not unnecessarily repeating actions and character behaviors you have already explored. You want, always, to be adding something new to what has come before, illuminating aspects of character and pushing the plot forward.

Is this the right place for the scene? Look at its place in the sequence of action surrounding it. It should arise out of what has come before and lead to what comes next.

■ Next, look at the scene in terms of the POV character

Who is this character, and what does he or she want? How much does the desire matter to the character? To the scene? Is the pulse of the scene strongly related to this desire?

What is his or her response to the event(s) of the scene? Is the response all interior, or can we also see it in the actions taken by the character?

If we are going to pull the reader into this scene, we have to have someone to care about. In a sense, we have to share the character's fate. *Do we?*

■ Identify the scene's problems

Does your scene have any of these problems? All of them can be "fixed" if the scene is basically strong.

■ No clear event

State the event you intended until you are satisfied that it is dramatic, significant, and large enough for a scene.

■ No clear beats of action

List those you can. Determine your intentions and write those beats. Now rewrite.

■ No clear viewpoint

Stick to one character's thoughts and feelings! When you are describing what other characters are doing, don't say what they are thinking; don't express their opinions except in dialogue. Let their behaviors speak for them. Then be sure you find ways to show your character reacting to actions and responding emotionally.

■ No clear goal/intention for the characters

So state one! Then see what you have to do to reshape the scene toward that goal. Is the goal thwarted or satisfied?

■ Or, conversely, **overly direct statement of purpose**; no subtext or subtlety

Don't give everything away too soon. Build a question into the first part of your scene, which the scene answers. If it doesn't, have you built suspense or muddiness?

■ Overwritten description and activity

For every line of description, ask yourself: How does this help the scene? What would happen if I took it out? Is it a cliché?

■ Or **insufficient grounding**

See your characters in place and time. Integrate lines of description into the action so that the reader sees them, too.

■ **Problems in dialogue:** banality; no difference between the voices of the characters; goes on too long; too direct

Write your dialogue on a new page, as if it is a play. No action or description. Just talk. How do you differentiate your characters? How do you develop them? Do they have certain habits of speech? Do they differ intellectually? Is one personality more volatile than the other? Knowing your character well will help you create apt dialogue. Then you can integrate it into the scene again.

■ Lacks focal point

Put a line down the middle of a page. On the left, list your beats of action. On the right, list the beats of emotion—moments of response. Look for ways to make these happen close to one another in a causally linked way. Make them accelerate in intensity and meaning. Find a place where the action can turn. Make sure your beats lead *up to* and then *away from* that point.

■ **Doesn't "add up":** we're not left in a different place from where we started

If this is true, you have to rethink the scene entirely. What is the scene supposed to be about? What should it mean for the characters, and for the story? Does the scene lack conflict, pulse, event?

14

SCENARIOS

A HELPFUL ACCESSORY TO PLANNING NARRATIVES

WRITE SCENARIOS AS AN ACCESSORY PRACTICE TO
READING SCENES AND TO PLANNING THEM.

- WHAT IS THE DIFFERENCE BETWEEN NARRATIVE SUMMARY
  AND SCENARIO WRITING?
- HOW IS A SCENARIO DEVELOPED?
- WHAT CAN YOU DO WITH SCENARIOS?

Defining the scenario

I have made frequent references to *narrative summary,* by which I
mean that part of a story in which the author tells the reader
what happened in compressed form. Such a passage may summarize a day, a week, a season, a year, or whatever. Narrative summary is especially common in novels, when the author wants to
cover a great deal of time economically, but it is also often the
basic fabric of a short story.

Here is a passage of narrative summary from my novel *Plain
Seeing:*

In Wichita Falls, the family piled into the back bedroom in
Tootie and Taylor's house. In a few days, Greta took a job pack-
ing flour for General Mills. She rented another tiny stucco house,
just inside the city limits at the far north side of the town. Opal
and Amos enrolled in school. Opal came home the second day all

excited. She had learned about the vocational program. After Christmas, when the new semester started, she could start a program that would send her, afternoons, into the hospital to learn lab work. She and Greta would both learn about buses—and patience—taking two or three each way every day. Greta worked rotating shifts, changing every two weeks. The midnight shift paid eight cents an hour more. Her regular pay was sixty-five cents an hour. On the railroad, she had worked for a dollar a day. She worked five and a half days a week. In six months, she'd get a raise. It was a union job. For the first time in her life, she could see the possibility of something beyond survival . . .

You can see that in some instances, what is a single sentence in the narrative summary could be rendered as a scene. For example, when the kids enrolled in school, a scene might have spelled out their anxiety about the large school and city kids. Or there could have been a scene detailing the day Opal came home from school excited about getting to work in the hospital through her school and showing her mother's reaction. I decided, however, that this passage should serve as a sketch of the family as it settled into a new place. This establishes information so that later scenes make sense. As a matter of economy and balance, there was no need to expand the summary.

There is another kind of passage, and I never knew quite what to call it until I read Elizabeth George's book on writing. She explains very well the idea of *dramatic narration,* in which the author conveys action in the story, leaving out dialogue, but telling the facts and action of what happened, and including elements of description, so that we do get some feel for the dramatic quality of the event. This differs from a scene in that it is not fully rendered; it is shorter, not moment to moment. As she points out, Jim Harrison uses this form of narration well and often. I have also used the term *summarized scene,* indicating its compression of a smaller unit of time, leaving out most dialogue, details of description, etc. I think George's term *dramatic narration* is similar, but can also cover a bit more ground.

You will recognize numerous examples, as you look for scenes, in which narrative is compressed except for perhaps a scrap of dialogue, but you do get a sense of the scene that might have been written. Again from *Plain Seeing,* embedded in a page that covers a summer, there is this short passage of *dramatic narration,* using George's concept:

> By the third [time], she was comfortable enough to pose, to flirt with the lens, to toss her hair. Willie had her jump from a low rock into the water, over and over, while he tried different angles. He shot from up close and from the other side of the pool. She lay down and brushed her hand through the water. He cooed and soothed and praised her; he talked so steadily, she never heard the camera clicking.

Now contrast that with a rendered scene that comes soon after the above passage, both of them about the character Lucy allowing her friend Willie to photograph her nude:

> So on another afternoon, when it seemed too hot to go out, he made gin rickeys for them, and then she took off her clothes and posed. The apartment had been made out of half of the first floor of a large house. It had a small kitchen and bathroom, but other than that, it was really just the open parlor and dining room, so the bed was where people had probably once sat to socialize, near the large bay window, jutting out toward the center of the room. There were three windows to make the bay, each with six panes of glass. There were sheer white curtains on the windows, and shades. She stood by the window nearest the bed and reached over to pull up the shade on the middle window. Then she pushed the curtain away from her slightly, to let the light in to fall on her. It was five in the afternoon, a Sunday. No one seemed to be out on the street. Somewhere a few houses away, an Edith Piaf record was playing. Still holding the curtain, she turned back to him, looking slightly over her shoulder, and

she said, "Something makes me so sad just now." She could feel
tears welling.

"Sundays are lonely," he said softly. He was on one knee, then
up again, shooting. "Beautiful, beautiful!" he exclaimed.

She dropped the curtain. He asked her to lean against it,
against the light. She would look like someone stepping out of a
halo, her image dark against light.

You can see the difference between the dramatic narration and
the scene in the *level of detail,* and in the consequent engagement
you feel with the character.

A scenario is an economical dramatic narration.

So a *scenario* could be an economical dramatic narration that you
intend to turn into a scene: *a functional summary of what happens,
with a sense of the feeling of the scene.* You wouldn't worry so much
about the beauty of the writing as you would about capturing
the important elements you want to remember. In the case of the
above scene, I happened to have written a scenario in my outline:

> Lucy and Willie meet in her apartment (describe) on a hot day
> to take photographs. It's a Sunday afternoon, with a lonely feel-
> ing to it. Lucy is feeling sad. As she sinks into melancholy reverie,
> Willie shoots pictures, saying that she is beautiful. He asks her to
> use the window and the curtain a certain way (this will be much
> like her memory of her mother's photos).

Obviously, this scenario is especially brief, because it is a short
scene, but for me, as I was planning the chapter in which it appears, it captured the event and tied it to its meaning (Lucy's
memory of her mother; this isn't stated in this scene, but it is else-
where). I do a lot of these brief plans just ahead of where I am in
my manuscript when I am writing a novel.

Developing a scenario

If you are writing a scenario as part of your planning, you would use it to pin down the *event and emotional meaning* of the scene, and you could describe *key actions*. Sometimes I list *beats* of action. Sometimes I write a few scraps of dialogue on the scenario page, usually something I think my characters will say at a climactic moment. I might write a phrase about an image I have in mind, or a reminder of something in an earlier scene to which I want to refer. If I have these things on paper, I don't have to hold so much in my head and so don't feel as rushed to write the scene to get it all down. The scenario used as a work tool is idiosyncratic, based on your preferred way of making notes.

Another way to use the scenario is to write it *after a draft, before you revise*. Let's say you have completed a chapter or a story, and you have an important, full scene with which you are not satisfied. Evaluate the scene; think about what you are trying to do in it. Then write a scenario before you do the revision. *Do not try to make the scenario match up with the scene you have already written.* The scenario is a summary of the scene as you want it to be. It is a "best-case summary." It will serve as a guide. There is no formula for how it should look or how long it should be. Some people think of it as a long paragraph, some as a page; obviously, the scenario of a novel would take a number of pages, but how many depends on you. When I wrote *Walking Dunes,* I wrote a scenario of a chunk at a time, usually writing around ten pages that turned into sixty to eighty pages of manuscript. For *A Chance to See Egypt,* I worked from a scenario that was only five pages long for the whole book and it served me well, but it was much less complicated than *Walking Dunes*.

If you are working on a novel, I urge you to do a scenario for each of your major scenes, at least a dozen of them. (I am thinking maybe half a page for each, or a note card.) Then look at what you have written and compare the settings, the time of day, events, and functions. You want variety, you want the sense of something building, and you want to avoid repeating yourself. (How many scenes take place in the kitchen?) Examining a dozen one-page scenarios with notes is a lot easier than examining a dozen scenes.

Telling yourself your scenario is both a test of the story and a celebration of it is a good way to start your writing day when you are in medias res. You won't lose the thread that way. You will, as John Gardner famously said, "enter the dream." It is Gardner's contention that the writer usually works intuitively, imagining a scene as part of that "dream" and quickly writing its significant aspects, trusting his instincts. Later, he looks at the scene objectively and revises in order to achieve "a totally convincing and elegant action." The scenario is one tool to help you reach that goal.

SAMPLE SCENES

I have included chapters from two of my novels, with comments about the functions of the scenes and some notes about how I developed them. Obviously, I could tell you things about my own scenes that I wouldn't know about another writer's work. I selected scenes that varied from one another but are transparent enough for you to see how they are constructed.

Go back to chapter 12, "Reading for Story and Scene," and select questions to guide your reading. Or select particular elements from other sections. For example, the first scene, from *More Than Allies*, is a "big scene," and you might want to glance over the section on that topic again before you read it. The selection from *Opal on Dry Ground* is an example of both negotiation and tension and of a clear shift in power. You might have "pulse" in mind or "character response" as you look at a particular sample scene.

Next you will want to read the two fine stories that follow my scenes and apply your new reading skills. I have chosen stories that should inspire and instruct you with their craft and, of course, the delight of the stories themselves.

Scene from *More Than Allies*

This is a whole chapter of the book, a "big scene" sequence in which there are a lot of characters and important action. Maggie and Dulcie are the young mothers of Jay and Gus; the boys are classmates in the fifth grade. The boy Hilario is older, the son of a friend of Dulcie's; his family is in the country illegally. The three boys have gotten into trouble together, and when it all erupts in this chapter, the two women find they have a lot more in common than they suspected. (Maggie is a substitute teacher. Dulcie is a maid. Both are separated from their husbands.)

A narrative summary opens and sets up the chapter. The scene actually begins when the women turn onto the street where the boys are and see a fire truck parked in the yard and a police car on the street with the three boys in the back. I've marked it with a star (★). The women's interaction with their sons is actually a short, cut-off scene; then the policeman comes and starts a new, long scene, marked with ★★. The next shift comes when the officer takes the women to their boys. Note how the scene makes a little turn when the policeman talks to Hilario. Can you get a mental picture of where people are in this scene? Marked with ★★★. The last scene is at the trailer; in the car we just have a paragraph of transition.

In each case, look for the arc of the scene, the way it is constructed, and what "work" the scene does in the chapter.

I would suggest using the first model from "Reading for Story and Scene" for your first analysis of this chapter. After that, you might go through the scene identifying the *action beats* to see how everything is integrated, and then go through it again to see how the *emotional beats*—Maggie is the POV character—are developed. These are like couplets of *action and reaction*. You could also go through the scene looking for the small physical ways that Maggie responds to pressure, such as when she and Dulcie clasp hands, or when she gets nauseated.

Everything that happens in this scene has some kind of precedent in an earlier scene, so there is a sense of things coming together or "coming to a head." The boys' behavior puts a lot of fresh pressure on both women to figure out how to improve their lives, and how to connect the boys with their fathers. Thus the pulse of the scene is linked to the overall pulse of the novel.

This was an important chapter in the book; a friend gave me the idea for it when I told her, "I need for my boys to get in some trouble that doesn't really hurt anyone." I drove around town until I found a perfect spot where something like this could happen, and I studied the layout, the slope of the landscape, etc., so that I could see how the action would take place. I worked out the beats of what the boys did and then of the scene with the cops and the mothers. Not all that action made it into the scenes, but the work gave my writing a solid base.

The boys were missing. Maggie had told Jay she wanted him home by two. It was past three, and there was no sign of him. She went to Dulcie's. They left a note on Dulcie's door and went off in Maggie's car to look in likely places. First they checked at Lupe's. Gus and Jay had come by for Hilario a little before noon, and they had gone off on their bikes (Hilario on the ancient one the station owner had lent him). From Lupe's, Maggie and Dulcie scouted spots along the creek, and the big ditch under the freeway near Maggie's house where, this time of the year, a thousand things were growing and sprouting and begging to be explored. They went by Rachel's house and Maggie ran in to see if Mason had seen them. Finally, Maggie said she had to get home. Jay was on his bike, it was only mid-afternoon, but she was angry with him for his tardiness. Dulcie said Gus and Hilario often spent the day away but conceded that Maggie had set a time. "I always want to know where he is," Maggie said, a little defensively. Dulcie said, "I used to be like that."

When Maggie went home again and told Polly where she'd been—she went in talking, before Polly could say anything about her being late—Polly immediately said, "But don't you think he—" and at exactly that same moment, Maggie realized where they would have gone. Jay would have something to show off, something to share. How stupid not to have thought of it in the first place.

"He has this spot where he liked to go with his dad last year."

She had asked Dulcie to ride over with her. "It's a pretty piece of property, not very far, but they don't have any business being there." She confessed that she had gone there herself earlier in the week, trying to cheer Jay up. "He looks at me a way, sometimes, it makes me want to scream. We have to get out of the house." Dulcie, maddeningly, said nothing.

At the intersection by the junior high, they had to wait for a line of a dozen or more bicyclists to pass. They were all dressed alike, in white helmets and T-shirts and lemon yellow tight shorts. They were in their fifties, maybe their sixties, trim as sticks, and Maggie was so fascinated, she let a car half a block away pass before she inched forward to turn. A driver behind her honked. "Okay!" she yelled, then glanced at Dulcie, who had no expression at all.

★As they turned onto the street where the Gabrelli property was, though, Dulcie whispered, "*Mother of God*. Not up there," pointing toward the Gabrelli house.

A fire truck was parked in the yard, and a police car at the street. Maggie pulled in beside the car and jumped out. The three boys were in the back, huddled like sick little birds on the seat. Maggie tried the door handle. Of course it was locked. She turned to Dulcie, but Dulcie wasn't behind her; she was still standing by the car, her hands covering her mouth. Jay saw Maggie. His eyes widened, and he started crying. His poor broken-out face was puffed and red. Gus glanced up, then hung his head. Hilario yawned and leaned against the back seat, as if this was all so boring. It was an act, Maggie thought, I bet he's scared to death.

She banged on the window. "What have you done?"

★★"Ma'am," someone said behind her. It was a policeman. She recognized him. He often sat at the busy intersection kids had to cross in the morning near the grade school. He had a round, friendly face and freckles. He was younger than she was. He looked like a kid trying to play grown-up, his face so serious, his shoulders pulled back bravely.

Another cop was striding across the yard toward them. The engine of the fire truck turned over, and Maggie jumped at the noise. Slowly, the truck pulled out and away. Whatever had been going on seemed to be over.

Dulcie had moved next to Maggie. At the same moment, they reached for one another, clasped hands, and squeezed hard.

As the second policeman approached, the first introduced himself—Officer Brandon—and suggested they step away from the car. Maggie glanced at her son, whose swollen face was glossy with tears, then followed the cop a few yards away, toward the farm house. What had been going on while she was eating eggplant caviar?

They're all right, she told herself. Nobody dies of crying. She ought to know!

"Are you the boys' mothers?" the officer asked.

Maggie nodded. He looked at Dulcie, who said, "Yes." The officer took out a pad and pen and took their names. Maggie was dressed up, from the lunch. Dulcie was wearing an old pair of jeans and a T-shirt. Maggie wished they were dressed more alike. She hoped Dulcie wasn't uncomfortable. Uncomfortable! Their kids were locked in a cop car.

"You knew they were here? You know this is private property?" The officer directed his question to Dulcie. Maggie tried to explain—Jay's dad had worked here in the summer, he had been told it was okay to play. The officer looked doubtful. He said, "We were about to take them to the station and give you a call. They're very lucky, you know, not to be hurt. You're very lucky. That's the thing, boys this age, playing unsupervised."

Maggie's cheeks felt scorched in the sun, under his scolding gaze. Did he really think mothers stood around and watched nine-year-old boys all day? "What happened?" she asked. She had a sensation of choking. She tried to swallow, but couldn't make her throat work. She panicked, for an instant, and then she squeezed Dulcie's hand again and made herself stop trying to swallow. "What did they do?" She glanced beyond the cop, toward the far part of the property. She didn't see any signs of a fire.

Officer Brandon explained that the boys had built a fire in the shed to roast hot dogs. They made some effort to put it out, but left it smoldering. Then they went up the slope where the abandoned cars were parked, to fool around. He shook his head. "Boys," he said. "They love cars." He shook his head again. "These old cars ought to be hauled away. You see 'em all over. I bet they've been here thirty years. Course, they're not expecting anybody to be trying a joy-ride in them, are they?"

From where they stood, Maggie couldn't see the police car. She thought the officer had deliberately placed them like that. It was a kind of torture. "They're not hurt?" she said. It required enormous effort to keep from crying. She wished she had brought Polly. Of course she couldn't have known there was going to be trouble. Of course Polly had her hands full with two babies.

"Oh," she said. She was nauseated. The ground seemed to be unstable beneath her feet. She wished Mrs. Cecil was there. A principal would know how to handle something like this. She'd know the boys hadn't meant any harm.

Dulcie put her arm around her shoulders. "They're okay," she said.

"The Mexican boy—the little one—" the police said. "He was in the car."

"Gus," Dulcie said.

"The other two pushed it off, a little roll off that slope, a little ride. The car hit the corner of the shed, glanced off that fallen roof, and slid to a stop." His look grew sterner. "Very lucky," he said. "It must have shook him pretty good, but it didn't do him any significant damage." He touched his chin. "Gave him a little nick here, the steering wheel. Maybe some bruises. We looked him over pretty good."

Maggie looked at Dulcie. She thought Dulcie had to be alarmed, but she kept her face utterly neutral, as if she had turned to stone.

"The impact of the car shook the shed roof, and some lumber shifted. The coals sparked. There was a fire."

"Oh God." Maggie tasted tuna and jalapeño and the sour tang of wine in her throat.

"It didn't amount to much. The neighbor across the road came out when he heard the car hit, and saw smoke. Called the fire department and us."

"The car?" Dulcie said. "It's wrecked?"

"The car's junk, ma'am. The car didn't matter. Old Willys, can you believe it? If somebody had taken care of it, it'd be worth something. Rusted out, though. Nothing worth salvaging." Maggie remembered Mo saying the same thing. Too bad, he said. He had always wanted an old car.

"And nothing burned?" Dulcie said.

"No, ma'am, few scraps of wood." Once again, he said, "Lucky thing." Maggie coughed. Her throat was hurting. He said, "Good thing we had that little rain this week, the grass has been so dry. Might have been quite a little brush fire, if things had gone badly."

"But they didn't," Dulcie said calmly. "Officer, can we take the boys?"

"One thing," he said. "The big kid. Whose kid is he? He won't say anything. He speak English?"

Dulcie said, "He's my sister's son. He's probably scared. Hilario Hinojosa. Of course he speaks English. He's bilingual." Maggie couldn't help staring at her, but Dulcie didn't pay any attention. Obviously, she had her reasons to lie.

"I think we better take him home," the policeman said.

"They're not home," Dulcie said quickly. "His parents aren't there. He's staying with me over the weekend."

He looked at her for a moment, one eyebrow raised slightly. "How's that?"

"They've gone to Salem," Dulcie said. "To see my mother."

He poised his pen over the pad. "What's their address, ma'am?"

"They're staying with me. They're just moving, so they're staying with me right now."

"I'm going to need to talk to his folks."

"Oh sure. Monday. They'll be back then."

He put the pad away. Maggie didn't think he was especially satisfied, but nothing Dulcie had said was unreasonable. Family did
stay with one another. Especially poor people, and he wouldn't
have any trouble thinking of Dulcie as poor. He didn't have any
reason to be suspicious. He didn't know two families couldn't fit
in Dulcie's place.

★★★They walked back to the car. The other policeman was
leaning against it, chewing on a toothpick. Jay called out. "Mom!"
Maggie's heart jumped. "Please," she said.

Officer Brandon opened the door and the boys crawled out
slowly. Jay threw his arms around his mother. Gus rubbed his eyes
and stood back. Hilario stood, his head cocked a little, his eyes
hooded and sullen and older than a boy's eyes should be.

Brandon said, "I'm going to let you boys go with your mothers now. You'll be getting letters. I think someone will want to
talk to you."

Jay clung to Maggie.

"And there'll be some damages."

"Oh God," Maggie said. "The car?"

"We're trying to get hold of the owners here. They're in Con-
cord, California. I imagine they'll want to have the car towed
away to the junk yard. I think you'll have to pay for that."

Dulcie said, "Of course."

"The shed—" He shrugged. "It's negligible. I don't know why
he's left it there."

"My bike," Gus said. They all turned toward him.

Officer Brandon made a sucking noise. "They're up by the
shed. Why don't you boys go get them and we'll put them in the
trunk?"

Maggie and the policemen stared at one another uncomfortably.
Dulcie got in the front seat of the car, leaving the car door open.

Jay's and Gus's bikes fit in the trunk, but of course it wouldn't
close. The second policeman rummaged and found a piece of
rope in the car. Hilario stood to one side with his hands on his
bike's handlebars. He still hadn't spoken since the women arrived.

"It's not far," Maggie said. "He can ride his bicycle."

"Yeah, okay," Officer Brandon said. The second policeman announced that the trunk was secure. He gave the lid a sound pat. Brandon looked like something was still bothering him.

"I go?" Hilario finally said. He had been following everything.

"You've got no business in a car," Brandon told him. "Next time I suppose you'll steal one that runs."

Hilario said, "Cabrón." Gus gasped.

The policeman said, "I don't speak Spanish, but I'm not stupid, kid. How old are you?"

Hilario said, "Thirteen."

"I could take you to juvey, you know. This could be a bigger thing."

Maggie didn't think Hilario understood. He stood still, but he didn't look cowed now, with his bike between his legs, his feet planted square in the dirt. "Thank you, mister," he said.

"Phht!" the policeman said. He turned and walked briskly back to his car and got in on the driver's side. Maggie and the boys hadn't moved. He leaned his head out of the police car. "Watch whose yard you fool around in," he said. "Somebody just might shoot you." He spun the wheels, digging out in reverse.

The boys rode in the back seat. Dulcie hadn't said anything to Gus, so Maggie thought, I can wait, too. I won't get all excited right now. She couldn't imagine what Polly would say. A fireman's grandson, starting a vandal's fire!

At the trailer, Dulcie said, "It sounds like it was Gus's fault. I'll pay for the towing."

"It wasn't my fault!" Gus said. Dulcie gave him a hard look.

"I'm sure it was Jay's idea," Maggie said. "Anyway, they did it all together."

"Lupe doesn't have any money," Dulcie said.

"No," Maggie said.

Dulcie shrugged. "Let's see what they say. What're they going to do? Put us in jail?"

It didn't feel right between them, Maggie thought. There was something she needed to say, but she didn't know what it was. "I'll talk to you," she said. Dulcie nodded, and walked into the trailer behind her son.

Questions

• Think about the presence or absence of overt conflict in this scene. You'll want to consider the issue of power. Clearly, the police are antagonists to Dulcie and Maggie, but from what position can the women protest? What do they do to protect the interests of their sons? How do Maggie's and Dulcie's attitudes differ? What experiences might account for the differences? Keep in mind that the town where the novel is set is a beautiful little community with a tourist-destination regional theater and a high median income.

• Maggie and Dulcie don't know each other except as parents of the boys. How are things left between them at the end of the chapter?

Scene from *Opal on Dry Ground*

My novel *Opal on Dry Ground* concerns Opal's relationship with her grown daughters, who have moved back in with her after her remarriage. In this chapter, Clancy, who is not married, but whose lover, Travis, wants to marry her, is having his baby. Opal, in her usual fashion, is right in the thick of things, trying to manage Clancy's childbearing.

Note the sequence of scenes in the chapter:

1. Clancy realizes she is in labor.

2. Small summary sequence leading into Clancy's "prep."

3. Clancy's escalating labor. It's getting harder and harder, and Opal just can't stand for her daughter to be in pain. After a whole lifetime of giving in to her mother's management, Clancy is finally going to seize control of her own life here—concerning something that matters so much, her own child. Watch the escalation of Clancy's pain, the escalation of Opal's interference, *and* the escalation of Clancy's sense of agency. You might also watch how the passage of the day is indicated in summary and in sentences of transition.

4. The actual delivery scene is very short, with a high pitch of tension and a quick release.

5. The last scene, the next morning, provides a release from tension, and Clancy's embrace of motherhood. It also signals a new possibility in her relationship with Travis, who, after all, was there for the baby's birth and who is the willing and loving father. You could say that the ending is both closed and open, depending on what you are talking about.

Clancy locks the door to the ladies' room at the bank and gets down on her hands and knees in the Dromedary Droop position. She raises her back, drops her head, and counts to five, then releases. She raises her back again.

It hurts too much. Whatever this is supposed to relieve is not relieved. The pain in her lower back has spread to her abdomen, and it is getting worse. It comes in waves, then balls up inside her and holds on. Then, in a little while, it comes again.

She isn't ready for this. She isn't ready to climb up on a table and spread her legs wide and grunt and moan and push. She isn't ready for a baby that cries and needs things all the time.

She'll be ready later. If she can rest first, she'll feel up to it. Not now, though. Now is too soon.

She goes back to her desk to call her doctor, and Opal.

"I called Travis's mother and she's going out to the field to get him," Opal says when they're checking into the hospital.

"I don't care," Clancy says from between clenched teeth.

"Oh!" Opal cries. She waves at the nurse behind the desk. "It hasn't been five minutes!" she says. "She's in *labor*."

"Yes, ma'am," the nurse says calmly. "We're going to take a look right now." She has a wheelchair for Clancy. "Give us half an hour," she tells Opal. "You're the grandmother?"

Of course Opal can't wait half an hour. Clancy has changed into a hospital gown and climbed up on the labor bed when Opal sticks her nose in. "What do they say?"

"Mama," Clancy says.

Behind Opal, Dr. Stone says, "Excuse, please," and pushes the door wide into the room.

"My mother," Clancy says. "Opal Duffy."

Dr. Stone shakes Opal's hand. "I'll just check her dilation, Mrs. Duffy." Gently he pushes Opal out and the door shut.

"You're in for some hard work, Clancy, but I don't foresee any complications," he says as he's taking off his glove.

"How long?" A cramp seizes her. She hopes he'll say, Let's go in and get it over with right now.

"It's going to be hours. I'm going to send in a little Jell-O for you; you try to rest. Is your—is the father coming into the delivery room?"

They've never discussed it. "I don't think so," she says. The thought of Travis in a hospital gown and mask makes her giddy. She doesn't think he'd want it.

When someone brings in a tiny bowl of orange Jell-O, Opal takes the spoon and tries to feed Clancy. "Don't be stupid, Mother," Clancy says. "I'm not sick." She also is not hungry, but she puts a lump of Jell-O in her mouth and savors its tart coolness on her tongue. She takes another and lets it slide down her throat. She is grateful for the distraction.

"Not yet, you're not," her mother says. Then she settles herself in the armchair and opens a magazine. "*You* tell *me* when you want me to do something," she says in a hurt tone.

"Mama," Clancy says, "just be here, okay? Just wait."

She tries to breathe right when the pains come, the way she read in her books. Now she wishes she'd gone to one of those classes where they practice, but you go to them in pairs, and she didn't want to take a partner. She didn't want to think about labor till she had to. Now she has to.

She moans loudly and Opal throws the magazine on the floor. "Should I get somebody?" she says.

"Mother, you've had two babies, don't you know anything?" Clancy says when she can. "It just has to *happen*."

"When I had you, they didn't stick you in a room to yell it out," Opal says. "They gave you something to help. Now you have to ask. Well, I can do that, can't I? I can find a nurse and make her do something about your pain."

"It's not pain, Mother," Clancy says with great effort. "It's—labor." And, oh, it hurts.

Before Opal can say anything more, Travis enters the room. "I couldn't get here sooner," he says. "I had to clean up."

"Nothing's happened yet," Clancy says, just before another pain. Travis looks stricken, as if she's been in an accident. "It's going to be hours." Suddenly she's so aggravated with them both, she says peevishly, "It takes *time* to have a baby."

"Maybe I'll go get some supper," Travis says. "Or should I stay?"

Clancy leans back on her elbows. "I think you should go, and take Mother with you, and let me rest, like Dr. Stone says. What can you do?"

"Leave you by *yourself*?" Opal says.

"Mama, I'm in the *hospital*," she says, but it sounds more like a moan. "And I'm really, really busy."

While they're gone an aide comes in with a razor. "What's that for?" Clancy demands. The woman says she's going to "prep" her. Clancy says, "Dr. Stone says I don't have to be shaved."

"Oh, dear, everyone is shaved," the nurse says. She pulls Clancy's gown up.

Clancy jerks it right back down. "I don't want to!" she says. "Dr. Stone says he can find his way through my hair!" she yells, and the aide laughs.

"Stubborn, aren't you?" she says, but she goes away.

Clancy lies back, exhausted and pleased. She remembers something one of the women at work told her. "Just remember, everyone expects you to make noise. Make a lot of it and they'll pay attention."

She smiles and rubs her belly. Maybe she can do this after all.

By the time Opal and Travis return, labor is steady and hard and takes all her attention. She has learned the pattern of the pains, though; she knows she can ride them out; she gets through the hard part because she knows she's going to slide down, down again, to rest. She's annoyed at her mother and Travis, standing around looking helpless; she wants to get on with this baby business, and something about their helplessness and their fussy looks makes her think they're holding things up. But somehow she never finds the energy to scold them, and when the pains are harder, after the nurse checks and says, "Good girl, you're two more centimeters dilated," she's glad for them, one on each side, squeezing her hand. They talk to each other over her body; she hears their voices but can't quite tell what they're saying. She hears the buzzing in her head she knows so well, only louder than it's ever been, and she hears the grunting sounds that seem to be coming from somewhere *over there,* although she knows they are sounds she's making, sounds she's never made before.

"Oh, oh," she cries in the late afternoon, "I can't stand it! I don't want to!"

"I'll get somebody," Travis says.

"It'd be better another time," she says most reasonable. "After I have a nap. Tomorrow. Tell them—oh, oh!"

The nurse brings her fresh ice chips and says it won't be much longer.

Clancy can't stand the pain in her back. She pulls herself up by Travis's arm, squeezing it with both hands. "I want to—turn over—" she manages to say.

Opal says, "You need some Demerol! Why haven't they given you anything?"

"I didn't want it—" she says. She doesn't want to feel fuzzy and crazy and lost.

Opal goes out and comes back with a nurse who has a needle.

"A pinch in the thigh—" the nurse says.

Clancy slaps her hand away.

"Clancy!" Opal says.

The nurse says, "She has to say."

Travis says, "Squeeze harder," taking her hand.

She has climbed up to a kind of squat. The nurse pulls guardrails up on the sides of the bed. She says, "They get in every sort of position these days." She's probably talking to Opal. Nurse to nurse.

Clancy brays. Travis wipes her forehead. In a moment she lies down again. "My feet are cold," she says. She's wearing cotton crew socks with her hospital gown. Travis begins rubbing her feet.

"C-cold," she chatters.

Travis falls back into a chair and pulls his shoes and socks off. He puts his socks over Clancy's.

"Travis!" Opal says. "She can't wear those."

"They're clean," he says. He wipes Clancy's face again.

"You need a shot," Opal says.

"I hate Demerol," Clancy says. She had it when she broke her ankle, years ago. She remembers still the panic she felt, even as she floated above it.

"Phenergan. I'll find the doctor. He can give you Phenergan."

Clancy, holding on to Travis, pulls herself up again. "Go away," she says to her mother. "Go wait somewhere while I—uh-uh—" She waits out the hardest pain yet, a long slope of it. Then she looks at her mother. "You think I can't do this, don't you? *You think you have to do it for me!*"

"Clancy!" Opal says.

"Go *away. This is my baby.*"

Travis turns away too. "Not you," Clancy says. "Not yet."

Opal, with a startled whimper, goes out of the room. Travis says, "What can I do, honey? What can I do?"

"My back," she moans. "Press—there—"

The pains are so bad, and fast. The nurse is in to check. It's time; she's going to have this baby.

Clancy leans into Travis. "My back," she moans again. And suddenly, he has climbed up onto the bed with her, behind her, and he straddles her, pressing her back and holding her arms, his long strong thighs warm against her legs. "You're going to have a baby," he says softly into her hair. "You're going to have my baby." He kisses her neck. "I love you, Clancy. Get used to it."

It's her baby, though, all hers, and when they wheel her into the delivery room, she leaves Travis behind. The doctor says, "Let it go, Clancy. Yell if you want, and *push!*" They jab a needle into her down there, but she doesn't feel it. *"Come on!"* she shrieks. *"It hurts!"* The nurse says *not now*, and then *now, push, push; "Fuck!"* Clancy yells. *"Whoo!"* she brays. *"Unhh! Fuck!"*

"Here it comes," the doctor says. "Look, Clancy, don't miss this!"

In the mirror, she sees the head crown. Her creamy baby slithers out. The doctor holds the baby up. Her eyes blur and she lays her head back. Someone puts the baby on her for a moment.

"It's a boy," someone says.

She touches his tiny hand. "I did it," she tells him. She means to be serious—*she has done something wonderful all by herself*—but she's laughing. The baby, solemn, waves his free fist. Clancy waves hers, too.

Then it's morning. She lies bathed and rested on her bed, and they bring the baby wrapped in a blanket. At the sight of him, her breasts pulse, and her womb. *This is her child.* Opal and Travis tiptoe in and stand, one on each side of the bed.

"It's a boy," Opal says reverently.

"He's got hair," Travis says.

"What'll we name him?" Opal asks. "After his daddy?"

Clancy looks at her mother, then at Travis, and then at the baby. She realizes that the buzzing in her head has gone away.

"His daddy, and mine," Clancy says. "Murphy Thatcher."

"This beats everything," Travis says. "This is the best yet."

Clancy doesn't say, but she agrees.

Questions

A good way to analyze the chapter is to pull out the "Clancy beats" first. Look at what she actually does, at what is happening to her. Everything else is a distraction and interruption of her work of having the baby. Opal interferes. Travis tries to be helpful, but he is clueless. You can see how they are threaded into the scenes, changing the rhythm of Clancy's labor but not gaining control of it. The chapter is all about her becoming the agent of her own life.

- What are the steps that Clancy takes in asserting herself in order to take command?
- What do you think is the focal point of the chapter?

"Shout" by Dagoberto Gilb

He beat on the screen door. "Will somebody open this?!" Unlike most men, he didn't leave his hard hat in his truck, he took it inside his home, and he had it in his hand. His body was dry now, at least it wasn't like it was two hours ago at work, when he wrung his T-shirt of sweat, making it drool between the fingers of his fist, he and his partner making as much of a joke out of it as they could. That's how hot it was, how humid, and it'd been like this, in the nineties and hundreds, for two weeks, and it'd been hot enough before that. All he could think about was unlacing his dirty boots, then peeling off those stinky socks, then the rest. He'd take a cold one into the shower. The second one. He'd down the first one right at the refrigerator. "Come on!" Three and four were to be appreciated, five was mellow, and six let him nap before bed.

"I didn't hear you," his wife said.

"Didn't *hear* me? How *couldn't* you hear me? And why's it locked anyways? When I get here I don't feel like waiting to come in. Why can't you leave the thing unlocked?"

"Why do you think?"

"Well don't let the baby open it. I want this door open when I get home." He carried on in Spanish, *hijos de* and *putas* and *madres* and *chingadas*. This was the only Spanish he used at home. He tossed the hard hat near the door, relieved to be inside, even though it was probably hotter than outside, even though she was acting mad. He took it that she'd been that way all day already.

Their children, three boys, were seven, four, and almost two, and they were, as should be expected, battling over something.

"Everybody shut up and be quiet!" he yelled. Of course that worsened the situation, because when he got mad he scared the baby, who immediately started crying.

"I'm so tired," he muttered.

She glared at him, the baby in her arms.

"You know sometimes I wish you were a man cuz I wouldn't let you get away with looks like that. I wouldn't take half the shit I take from you." He fell back into the wooden chair nobody sat in except him when he laced the high-top boots on, or off, as he already had. "You know how hot it was today? A hundred and five. It's unbelievable." He looked at her closely, deeply, which he didn't often do, especially this month. She was trying to settle down the baby and turned on the TV to distract the other two.

"It's too hard to breathe," he said to her. He walked barefooted for the beer and took out two. They were in the door tray of the freezer and almost frozen.

"So nothing happened today?" she asked. Already she wasn't mad at him. It was how she was, why they could get along.

"Nothing else was said. Maybe nothing's gonna happen. God knows this heat's making everybody act unnatural. But tomorrow's check day. If he's gonna get me most likely it'll be tomorrow." He finished a beer leaning against the tile near the kitchen sink, enjoying a peace that had settled into the apartment. The baby was content, the TV was on, the Armenians living an arm's reach away were chattering steadily, there was a radio on from an apartment in a building across from them, Mexican TV upstairs, pigeons, a dog, traffic noise, the huge city out there groaning its sound—all this silence in the apartment.

"There's other jobs," he said. "All of 'em end no matter what anyways."

It was a job neither of them wanted to end too soon. This year he'd been laid up for months after he fell and messed up his shoulder and back. He'd been drunk—a happy one that started after work—but he did it right there at his own front door, playing around. At the same time the duplex apartment they'd been living in for years had been sold and they had to move here. It was all they could get, all they were offered, since so few landlords wanted three children, boys no less, at a monthly rent they could afford. They were lucky to find it and it wasn't bad as places went, but they didn't like it much. They felt like they were starting out again, and that did not seem right. They'd talked this over since they'd moved in until it degenerated into talk about separation. And otherwise, in other details, it also wasn't the best year of their lives.

He showered in warm water, gradually turning the hot water down until it came out as cold as the summer allowed, letting the iced beer do the rest.

She was struggling getting dinner together, the boys were loud and complaining about being hungry, and well into the fifth beer, as he sat near the bright color and ever-happy tingle of the TV set, his back stiffening up, he snapped.

"Everybody has to shut up! I can't stand this today! I gotta relax some!"

She came back at him screaming too. "I can't stand *you*!"

He leaped. "You don't talk to me like that!"

She came right up to him. "You gonna hit me?!" she dared him.

The seven-year-old ran to his bed but the other two froze up, waiting for the tension to ease enough before their tears squeezed out.

"Get away from me," he said trying to contain himself. "You better get away from me right now. You know, just go home, go to your mother's, just go."

"*You* go!" *You* get out! We're gonna stay!"

He looked through her, then slapped a wall, rocking what seemed like the whole building. "You don't know how close you are."

He wouldn't leave. He walked into the bedroom, then walked out, sweating. He went into the empty kitchen—they were all in the children's room, where there was much crying—and he took a plate and filled it with what she'd made and went in front of the tube and he clicked on a ball game, told himself to calm himself and let it all pass at least tonight, at least while the weather was like it was and while these other things were still bothering both of them, and then he popped the sixth beer. He wasn't going to fall asleep on the couch tonight.

Eventually his family came out, one by one peeking around a corner to see what he looked like. Then they ate in a whisper, even cutting loose here and there with a little giggle or gripe. Eventually the sun did set, though that did nothing to wash off the glue of heat.

And eventually the older boys felt comfortable enough to complain about bedtime. Only the baby cried—he was tired and wanted to sleep but couldn't because a cold had clogged his nose. Still, they were all trying to maintain the truce when from outside, a new voice came in: SHUT THAT FUCKING KID UP YOU FUCKING PEOPLE! HEY! SHUT THAT FUCKING KID UP OVER THERE!

It was like an explosion except that he flew toward it. He shook the window screen with his voice. "You fuck yourself, asshole. You stupid asshole, you shut your mouth!" He ran out the other way, out the screen door and around and under the heated stars. "Come on out here, mouth! Come out and say that to my face!" He squinted at all the windows around him, no idea where it came from. "So come on! Say it right now!" There was no taker, and he turned away, his blood still bright red.

When he came back inside, the children had gone to bed and she was lying down with the baby, who'd fallen asleep. He went back to the chair. The game ended, she came out, half-closing the door behind her, and went straight to their bed. He followed.

"I dunno," he said after some time. He'd been wearing shorts and nothing else since his shower, and it shouldn't have taken him so long, yet he just sat there on the bed. Finally he turned on the fan and it whirred, ticking as it pivoted left and right. "It doesn't do any good, but it's worse without it." He looked at her like he did earlier. "I'm kinda glad nobody came out. Afterwards I imagined some nut just shooting me, or a few guys coming. I'm getting too old for that shit."

She wasn't talking.

"So what did they say?" he asked her. "At the clinic?"

"Yes."

"Yes what?"

"That I am."

They both listened to the fan and to the mix of music from the Armenians and that TV upstairs.

"I would've never thought it could happen," he said. "That one time, and it wasn't even good."

"Maybe for you. I knew it then."

"You did?"

She rolled on her side.

"I'm sorry about all the yelling," he said.

"I was happy you went after that man. I always wanna do stuff like that."

He rolled to her.

"I'm too sticky. It's too hot."

"I have to. We do. It's been too long, and now it doesn't matter."

"It does matter," she said. "I love you."

"I'm sorry," he said, reaching over to touch her breast. "You know I'm sorry."

He took another shower afterward. A cold shower. His breath sputtered and noises hopped from his throat. He crawled into the bed naked, onto the sheet that seemed as hot as ever, and listened to outside, to that mournful Armenian music mixing with Spanish, and to the fan, and it had stilled him. It was joy, and it was so strange. She'd fallen asleep and so he resisted kissing her, telling her. He thought he should hold on to this as long as he could, until he heard the pitch of the freeway climb, telling him that dawn was near and it was almost time to go back to work.

Questions

This is a compact, muscled story that takes place all on one hot evening. It presents a family both *as they are* and *as they are on this night*. Can you make this distinction? Can you find the ways that the author does?

The second reading model, "Scene Analysis," might be useful to you in talking about the story as a whole. Then study the structure of the story, with its scenes and exposition. Identify what you consider to be the most important moments in the story, and then see how a scene is built around each. Sometimes what doesn't happen is the important element in the scene. Both of these characters are living under pressure; their marriage is, in effect, a third fulcrum, and the one we see in the forefront of the story. Notice the ways that the author firmly sets these things into a world. How is the story embedded in the sense of a larger story (of family, community, etc.)?

Can you see the story as one of "release of tension"? Or of "negotiation"? How else might you describe the arc of its events? Identify a line of tension and release and list its beats; there will be more than one such line.

Advanced Scene Exercise

Think of a situation in which two characters have reached a point of high tension. You will have to imagine the reason for their conflict. Write a brief summary of their quarrel, just a few sentences, for your own use.

Enter the target scene very late in the conflict, at the point where one of the two characters has walked away from the other in order to deflect the tension. (Your characters don't have to be spouses, as in Gilb's story.) Don't assume the reader knows anything before this. Show this character physically "working off" the tension, or at least attempting to do so. Then introduce a new element in the scene, coming from outside the scene so far. This could be the arrival of a new character, a call, a baby crying, something happening outside the room, etc. Show the effect of this new element on the focus character.

Take the response of the character only a few beats and then cut off the scene at a high point. Leave the reader wondering what will happen next.

FOLLOW-UP

If this scene exercise appealed to you, go ahead and write the scene sequence:

- The quarrel, ending with one of the characters walking away

- The "working-off tension" scene, ending a few beats after the introduction of an outside element that changes the dynamics of the situation

- A scene that picks up immediately after the working-off tension scene and has the character dealing with the new element, or that puts the original two characters back together again at a later time. This might be when they resolve their quarrel; it might be after they have already resolved it (skipping time); it should be a definite change of tone.

"Cartography of a Heart" by Gina Ochsner

Because O'Neil's heart had been skipping and had threatened to give up altogether, the doctors decided to give him a new one. O'Neil was not a very important man. He had fought in a war, an unpopular one, and had in fact already nearly died several times. For these reasons and a few more he would have been hard-pressed to name, O'Neil was tempted to call off the replacement procedure. But the doctors insisted. After they took a lot of pictures, measuring with ultrasound to determine the exact size of heart they were looking for, they discovered that they'd never seen anyone with a heart like his, a heart of such unusual shape. This discovery aroused a certain amount of scientific interest in the cardiology unit, and the doctors wondered if anyone else in the city could also be carrying such an odd-shaped heart.

How his heart got into such a state, O'Neil couldn't figure. He had been in love once. It was a good love affair and innocent, confined to the realm of hand-holding and quick stolen kisses. And when he was drafted and sent to Vietnam, O'Neil only allowed himself to think of Marianne, to savor the thought of her at night when the ordinary daytime sounds crossed the boundary into nighttime noise and he could have his thoughts to himself. In this way he stretched the memory of Marianne, rationing her out to fill the nights of an entire tour.

But when he returned home, Marianne was gone—dead, her parents told him, of food poisoning. The sheer stupidity, the terrible irony of her dying instead of him bore down upon O'Neil like the sudden pressure he'd feel just before a nosebleed, only this pressure was in his heart, pushing on the chambers of his heart. That was the first time he had really taken any notice of his heart. But after that, it seemed to pain him on strange occasions for no particular reason: at his kid brother's wedding, after eating summer sausage, at his father's funeral, and once, in a movie theater. At first he was embarrassed, but after a while his discomfort outweighed his shame and finally he made an appointment at the VA hospital.

Later, when he came in to view his X-rays, the cardiologists, Dr. Gatlin and Dr. Moore, told him it was no wonder his heart wasn't cooperating with him. His heart was an anomaly, they said. Anomaly wasn't a word O'Neil cared for much because it hinted at trouble, suggested a huge fuck-up was in the works, or a nightmare that had patiently grown wings and was now waiting to hatch.

But the doctors were right: O'Neil's heart was kidney-shaped and abnormally large, with the muscle itself nearly twice the size of an ordinary man's. The chambers of the heart, however, were unusually small, so small that Dr. Gatlin wondered how O'Neil's heart managed to move his blood around at all. When the doctors showed him this, the darkened images on the film made darker against the white light, O'Neil thought of the ten thousand eggs of his youth, the generous pats of butter on his bread and dollops of cream in his coffee, and silently cursed.

Even worse, O'Neil would need a heart that was very much like his present one as his rib cage, sternum, and interior musculature had over time reshaped themselves to accommodate that strange heart. An ordinary heart would not do, Dr. Moore explained to O'Neil, as he had noted over the years how the whole of the body so often and fatally rebels against its parts. In the meantime, the doctors sent O'Neil home with a panic alert that would ring into ER and told him to rest easy, to wait, to try not to vex or agitate his unusual heart.

Finding a perfectly fitting heart proved to be even harder than the doctors thought it would be. For several months O'Neil waited, trying not to think about the tightness in his chest or about the person who would have to die in order for him to have a new heart. But when the phone rang beside his bed one afternoon he knew before he even picked up the receiver that it was the hospital calling, that someone, the right someone, had at last died.

The day of the surgery broke over the flat skyline of the city. O'Neil took a cab to the hospital. It was the dead of summer and already the air had run to humid, though it was still early morning. O'Neil waited in the visitors' lounge and trained his eyes on the ceiling where the overhead fans beat the air. Looking at them made him feel a little off-kilter, a little like slipping out of himself because each of the fans sliced the air at different speeds, and for an instant he felt as if he were back on the airfield, on the tarmac, watching the rotors spin, the slow wind-up dance to the tune of the turbine's whine and drone. He couldn't help looking at fans, ceiling or otherwise, lawnmowers, blenders, helicopters—anything with blades—without feeling a sense of danger and the taste of his fillings in the back of his mouth. He remembered a guy from his unit who dismounted from his chopper, leaving the rotors running. Who knows what he was thinking about—his wife, his kids—or maybe he just remembered something he'd left in the cockpit. But he turned around sharp and walked into the tail rotor, which neatly sliced his face from his head.

O'Neil had never seen a man without a face, and the oddest thing about the incident was that the man, who had a funny name like Emil or Emile but whom everyone called Eddy, went on to survive in spite of himself. O'Neil had gone to visit Eddy out of respect and curiosity, and though it was clear that it pained him, Eddy would talk with O'Neil, telling about the whirlpool baths the nurses used to remove the scars of the burn patients, the new plastic nose the doctors were designing for him, how it would clip in and attach just under the bones of his forehead. They'd trade gossip about the men in the burn ward, the men in the psych wards, and the women they had loved and wanted to love. This is when Eddy would invariably mention his wife, a woman O'Neil categorically disliked. That she took the kids and left her husband while he was still in the hospital seemed to O'Neil an expired cliché, an expected joke made no less cruel by its anticipation. She couldn't live with a man she couldn't look at, Eddy carefully explained during O'Neil's last visit, moving his mouth slowly so as not to open the healing scab that was his new face. She couldn't live with a face that couldn't be kissed.

Then O'Neil had told Eddy the story of the Emperor who had no skin. Of all the skins offered to him by beautiful princesses wishing to be chosen as his new bride, the Emperor picked the princess who brought the skin of her dog, for he had always wanted a tail to wag. This had made Eddy laugh, a strange sound at the back of his throat, and listening to it made O'Neil's chest go tight and his heart turn leaden. A nurse in crisp whites had come in then, whisking the privacy curtain around the steel semi-circular curtain rod and O'Neil had left, his chest hurting. If all a man wanted was to love and be loved, why couldn't he have it? he had wondered as he waited for the elevator.

The nurse called O'Neil's name and ushered him into pre-op where he exchanged his clothes for a gown that fastened in the front with tiny black Velcro dots. Then he was wheeled to the service elevator and down to the surgery staging area where a different nurse, green face mask and all business, dropped a cc of painkiller into his IV and wheeled him into the operating room. O'Neil, now groggy and feeling not a particle of pain in his chest, considered telling Doctors Gatlin and Moore the story of the Emperor's skin, the story of Eddy's face, and wondered if he would ever hear the story of the owner of the used and unusual heart beating in the ice chest on the gurney next to him.

Afterward, when the new heart was in place, his chest felt tender and there was a certain amount of pink scar tissue raised at the surgical site, but all in all O'Neil felt good and his chest light. When it was certain his body would not reject the perfectly fitting heart, his thoughts turned again to the Emperor, the unconventional gift of the wild princess, and he wondered what other changes this heart would bring. He had heard rumors from other heart transplant patients—of strange dreams, ghost pains and twitches, reminders of lost parts and donors.

The doctors sent him home with anticoagulants and new batteries for the panic pager, and every week O'Neil went in to see the doctors and answer their routine questions. For a long while he felt he was disappointing Dr. Gatlin and Dr. Moore.

"Any trouble breathing—shortness of breath?" Dr. Gatlin would ask, the stethoscope to O'Neil's chest.

"No."

"Any tightness or heaviness in your chest or arms?"

"No."

His favorite question: "How is your sex life?"

When Dr. Gatlin got to this one, O'Neil would roll his eyes to the ceiling and shrug.

But then one day, a day in spring when the birds were reclaiming the sky, O'Neil awoke feeling different, different somehow in his heart. He took the bus downtown and sat outside smoking. There was no denying the strange kick in his chest and the blood coursing differently through his veins, and he realized that he had a great and natural desire to love someone with his new heart.

He walked to a corner café that sometimes sold day-old donuts for half price and slid into a booth. And then he saw her: the woman for whom his new heart had been beating all these months. He knew it from the way the gait of her walk behind the counter matched the contractions in his ventricles. O'Neil followed her with his eyes, noted the curve of the back of her neck, the way her rib cage sank into her hips as she held a coffeepot in one hand and read back a phone order to the cook. He sat in the booth and studied her, her light talk and chatter, and tried to think of things he could say, something funny that might make her want to seat him in her section next time he came in.

Then he thought of Eddy again, whom he hadn't visited in a while, and thought how Eddy probably wanted to love someone, too. O'Neil wished that he could close his eyes and pray that God would give Eddy a new face. If he could have a new and perfect heart, then why couldn't Eddy have a new and perfect face? But even as he thought the words, he stopped himself. What was God supposed to do about it? Make a movie star face sprout out of Eddy's head, just like that?

Just then the waitress walked toward his booth, coffeepot in hand. He could tell that she was young, probably too young for him. But he remembered Eddy, thought of the regrets and fear that had held both of them back, and O'Neil decided to do what Eddy could not. And so he smiled, said something half witty, and decided if she showed an ounce of interest to pursue her with the ardor he should have pursued all the other women whom he wanted to love and wished had loved him in return.

In time, O'Neil and the waitress became lovers. Her name was June and she smelled like apples and sometimes like mint. He liked her because with her freckles she reminded him a little of Marianne. She would retell the stories of her day—the customers, their smells, how much they tipped, and with whom the cook was flirting—could tell these stories without pause, her talk an endless flow without a vein. She moved into his apartment, carrying a beat-up red suitcase and a small wire cage with a yellow canary named Petey inside. Petey's chirping filled his tiny kitchen with happy yellow noise, and O'Neil was glad for the combined noise of Petey and June for it kept him from thinking too often of Eddy, or of wondering too much about all those noises his donor had loved and left behind.

The simplicity of it, the ease with which their love fell into a simple rhythm, comforted O'Neil, who was learning to appreciate the occasional anomaly and had noted that too few things in life were simple anymore. Every night, when her shift was over, he would rub June's neck and then her feet, pushing the skin around the ankles and kneading the thick skin of her heels.

"You're an angel," June said to him one night, mid-story while he was rubbing.

"No I'm not. I've done things, some of them bad," O'Neil said, sliding his hand to the back of her neck, the place where her head and neck joined, and laying his head on her chest. He could hear then past her constant chatter, and as he did, listening very carefully to June's heart, he discovered that there was nothing there. He closed his eyes and held his breath, listening again for her heart, and exhaled at last when he heard a steady beat. He kissed her then, his forefinger at her throat checking her pulse, just to be sure.

That night they made love; a nondescript expression for O'Neil punctuated by the realization that even then, even as he was loving her, his heart did not beat any faster. Not with excitement, not with danger or mere lust, not with anything at all. Afterward he sat watching June paint her toenails, sat and smoked one cigarette after another, thinking that maybe because his heart had become so steady this meant he had finally matured and this love he felt for June, though not exciting, was a better kind of a love, his heart a better heart than the one before.

On an ordinary day that O'Neil had thought would unspool exactly as the day before, he awoke to the sound of Petey squawking and making strange clicking noises. June was at the mirror penciling in her eyebrows. He could tell from the quick deliberate jerks she was making with the pencil that she was mad at him, and he knew a fight was brewing. When June picked a fight, O'Neil would close his eyes and imagine June was Marianne and imagine what he would have said to Marianne. He'd imagine them both throwing their arms up at the same time at some point in the argument and laughing, laughing so hard they'd cry, and crying so hard they'd forget what it was they were fighting about. That was how it was supposed to work, O'Neil had always thought. But then June advanced, one hip jutted in her coffeepot pose, a pose of an older woman unafraid of a fight. O'Neil practiced deep breathing techniques the nurses told him to use when he felt stressed and waited for June to start in.

"You have the paper eyes of a face that can't be read, a heart that can't be touched," June said, tapping the place where his chest hair had grown back with her long eyebrow pencil sharpened to a point.

No, O'Neil wanted to protest, *not an untouchable heart, only a new, unknown heart*. But he knew she was right, that it couldn't work, and the thought was painful, right down to the capillaries.

"I can't live with a man who can't be loved," June said, and O'Neil bit his tongue and counted his breaths, thinking of the Emperor and wondering if any of the beautiful princesses had refused him because of his strange condition and what the Emperor would have said to them if he had been given the chance. That was the problem with tales—they hinted at a truth that wasn't actually there, a truth that was conditional on the belief that the human heart was noble, had great capacity for love, for loving the ugly and unlovable when one look at a guy like Eddy, at a guy like O'Neil even, would show that it just wasn't so. Not in this world.

When O'Neil had counted to twenty, he swallowed. "OK," he said at last, and he meant it. He was OK with it all—with June leaving him and her reasons why. But his heart dropped a notch in his chest, seemed to lurch and tip, and the steady strong rhythm he had enjoyed since the operation faltered and skipped to an uneven one-two punch beat. As she left with her red suitcase with the bad clasps, O'Neil noticed her clothes were leaking out and wondered if her suitcase might be bleeding. He held Petey in his cage out to her and watched her lug her suitcase and the bird down the narrow steps outside their apartment, each bump of the suitcase and squawk from Petey an arrow to his heart, and wished she would at least let him help her. *Is this what he would have had with Marianne?* he wondered. Is this what he had avoided? And for some reason the thought made him very sad, for he would have liked to have known for sure.

All the rest of the day he could feel himself unraveling inside and thought about using the panic alert. He actually thought then, too, that he missed his old heart, that bruised lump of muscle with the hardened arteries, which in all the days of crossing canyons and rivers and entire jungles had never given him this kind of trouble.

O'Neil opened the kitchen window and listened to the angry

clicks of June's shoes on the sidewalk below. He could tell by the way her footfalls sounded like sharp slaps that she was mad—mad in her heart, mad that he had hurt her somehow without either of them even noticing it until now. He leaned on the sill to catch the last glimpse of her disappearing around the corner. Outside on the street two lovers sat on the stoop holding hands and exchanging glances. Looking at them made O'Neil's chest hurt and he wanted to shout: *Stop! You are making a big mistake!* But as he watched them, his hand still at the panic button, he noted the care with which the man tucked a long strand of hair behind the woman's ear and realized that he might be witnessing something rare, that this couple might make it, might be two of those movie-of-the-week love story lovers who risk everything to save their love even as the world turns to fire and ash around them, and he couldn't help hating them a little for it.

O'Neil imagined that his heart, now pierced like St. Ambrose's, pierced like an old carnival target, was leaking at the edges. He closed his eyes and considered asking God to do a quick mend when he felt it: a tiny pocket of buoyancy in his chest. He felt it quickening, a bubble lodging in his heart, while outside the kitchen window he could see the flatiron sky hemmed in ten thousand stitches of light.

"So this is it," he said, clutching his chest and sliding against the refrigerator into a sitting position. He thought he'd hear more sound: bombs falling, the whistle of explosives. He worked the panic pager off his belt loop and lobbed it into the kitchen sink. His breath was coming in short gasps now, and in the pauses he thought he could hear the quiet whirring of his heart, that noise the washer makes on spin cycle just before the final click and pause.

Questions

You might start by using the third reading model. Consider the story itself as a whole first: its effect on you, the source of its power, the arc of the narrative. O'Neil is a character whose inner life is much more interesting than it appears; the story lets us inside.

Have you ever had something on your mind that made everything else in your life take on a different meaning, a different level of importance? Can you imagine a character in such a situation?

Now consider the way the story is constructed, in a narrative flow that is much like a tale or chronicle: This is what happened to a man with an anomalous heart. Overall, you have a story with a straightforward chronology in which a second story (with June) is embedded in that chronology, and in which the past hovers emotionally and is represented through O'Neil's images of and reflections on the past and the way it makes him feel now.

When you are ready to study the story for the way the author has used scenes, these questions can get you started:

- What scenes from the past impinge on the way O'Neil assesses his present life? Why do you think the author chose not to present Marianne in any scenes? (Consider the economy of the short story, as well as any thematic considerations.)
- Look at the way the scene with Eddy in the hospital is embedded in a larger, present-time scene. Do you see how, in the next section, the scene picks up again at the hospital where O'Neil is awaiting surgery?
- Look at the scenes with June, how they are linked into a sequence with its own structure: a beginning, middle, and end. What effect do you think this kind of strong structure within the narrative has on the story? (As opposed, say, to just telling us about June, as he does Eddy.)
- Examine the final scene for the way the author deftly places O'Neil firmly in the setting so that you can see him and not just hear the voice of his thinking. Do you think this is an example of a scene where what happens physically and what happens emotionally are the same thing?
- Look back over the story and watch for places where fragments or hints of scenes appear in the narrative. Do you get a feeling for the scenes that might have been written? (I'm

not saying they should have been, by any means; I'm saying that you can glean a lot from an image or bit of summarized action about things that happen "off the page.")

Advanced Scene Exercise

Reread the passage that begins with the first real scene: "The day of the surgery broke over the flat skyline of the city." Now, loosely following the pattern of the passage, write a scene with an embedded flashback. The pattern would be this:

- Put your character in a situation under pressure. Your first few sentences are scene summary, bringing the character into the setting.
- When you open the scene, have the character observe the setting. Something in the setting reminds him of a place or person in his past; switch then to the flashback of that old memory—an incident involving the person or place.
- When you have written the flashback, bring the reader back into the present scene. You can do this in one of two ways:
  - **a.** Simply cut to the present time again and pick up the present scene, with a comment that links the past and present.
  - **b.** Have the character note something in the setting again as a way to ground the scene in the present, and then continue the scene.

FURTHER READING

LIZZIE BRIGHT AND THE BUCKMINSTER BOY
by Gary D. Schmidt
Newbery Honor Book
Based on the sad and shameful destruction of an island community in 1912 Maine, Schmidt's lyrical, evocative novel for grades
six through ten thoroughly captivated me as well. Turner Buckminster is the son of a rigid preacher; his family moves from
Boston to a small town, where Turner is at a loss until he becomes friends with a black girl from nearby Malaga Island.
There's subtle humor, grace, and pain, but also a desolate climax.
I commend the book for its excellent structure not only to those
interested in young adult literature, but to beginning novelists
who can see how plot elements are woven and scene sequences
developed in a straightforward, satisfying way.

Schmidt is well into the story before he departs from straight
scenes to convey the passage of time with summary transitions.
Watch for these passages at the openings of chapters, as well as
the other ways he launches new scenes.

CATHERINE, CALLED BIRDY *by Karen Cushman*
Newbery Honor Book; ALA Notable Children's Book
For ages twelve and up, this book is fun for anyone interested in
the life of a thirteenth-century English girl. Her fictive diary is
clear-eyed and critical, filled with details of daily life and her efforts to avoid marrying the suitors vying for her hand.

Cushman does a great job of evoking the time and uses lots of descriptive passages. Watch how she does this in a way that is woven in with eventful scenes. Scenes are quite short, but accrue beautifully. See also *The Midwife's Apprentice*.

THE SMELL OF THE NIGHT by Andrea Camilleri

Sixth in a series starring engaging Inspector Salvo Montalbano and the landscape of his beloved Sicily. There's melancholy and off-page violence, but Salvo loves the folk, his lunches, the land, and a good mystery. I recommend this short book because it's structured entirely of scenes, with lots of good dialogue and variety in the openings. Read a little, and if you think you'll like him, read for fun, then study. Figure out which scenes are plot-pushers and which are part of his personal life subplots. See how he varies his settings and keeps things lively without ever getting violent.

CHILD OF MY HEART by Alice McDermott

Now we move to National Book Award author McDermott's bittersweet observation of a fifteen-year-old's summer on Long Island with a passel of kids to mind. Theresa's voice is cheerful, wry, precocious. The action is languid but so richly textured you will be amazed at just how much "plot" it turns out to have. Interestingly, the novel has no breaks. It is one long narrative, full of scenes and the narrator's commentary.

The opening pages provide background summary and then the rest of the book has a sense of vivid immediacy. You will learn a lot if you go through and identify what you consider to be the key scenes: those that set up important details for what will eventually happen; those that introduce relationships and build them; those that escalate the main lines of drama (the child's illness, Theresa's interactions with an aging painter). Make a kind of plot outline in this way, and then look for how she builds all the movement between those scenes with the smaller scenes that at first appear to be so gentle and static.

Consider how the author builds a strong sense of the location. How does she help you visualize East Hampton? Find specific scene elements that accomplish this. Be especially aware of how the descriptions arise from the activities of the characters.

Study the scene between Theresa and the artist. Does it disturb you? What do you think of the way the author built the scene? What "beats" are missing, and why?

You could spend a lot of time studying this short novel and come away both awed at McDermott's skill and armed with at least some ideas about how scene sequences work. Nothing will do, though, but for you to read the book several times and then do the hard work I've outlined above. It would be great if you could do it with another writer or a group. McDermott has said she is dismayed at the idea of craft books, but I'm sure she won't mind you reading her novel!

Lost in the City: Stories *by Edward P. Jones*
Jones, who won the Pulitzer Prize for his novel *The Known World,* set the fourteen stories of this collection in a black neighborhood of Washington, D.C., thirty to forty years ago. His characters are poor and their lives are sometimes dangerous and rife with degradation, but they are survivors, too, who demonstrate grit and hope. I'd emphasize that the real strength of the collection is that these characters are people who happen to be black, rather than stories about race. Their lives have a universality that will touch you deeply. Some of the stories are more like tone poems, but most are solid examples of fine story writing and well worth studying.

"Marie," excerpted earlier, gets all my stars. It has such memorable moments you'll want to figure out how he made them happen. Marie is a feisty old woman who is "up to here" with bureaucracy—enough that she slaps the rude receptionist in the Social Security office. With equal élan, she stands up to a mugger. This is solid storytelling and it requires strong scenes, each of them well structured and paced.

Look especially at "The Girl Who Raised Pigeons," "The Night Rhoda Ferguson Was Killed," and "The Sunday Following Mother's Day." You'll see a weaving of summaries, transitions, and scenes, some short, some lengthier.

BREATHING LESSONS *by Anne Tyler*
Winner of the Pulitzer Prize

Tyler limits the action of her novel to a single day in the life of an ordinary couple, their friends, and their family. She makes generous use of flashbacks to get around the limited structure, and she uses literal side trips on the journey that is the heart of the novel. Maggie and Ira Moran are traveling to the funeral of a friend.

There are three sections. The first and third are from Maggie's point of view, but they differ stylistically, since the last section provides a history of the relationship of Maggie's son, Jesse, to his father, Ira, and to his own son's mother, Fiona. Watch for the different types of interiority in these two sections.

The middle section is from Ira's point of view and is crisper. Take a scene from the first section and one from the second section and compare them in terms of the closeness of beats of action, the kind of interiority, the use of flashback, and other ways that the present action is or is not interrupted.

In the first section, choose a scene sequence such as the rear-ending of the old man on the road, and list the beats of action. This section is almost like a little story all its own. Note the way that Maggie's fury shifts when she sees who the driver is. How much does the author "tell" you about her feelings? How does she "show" you the shift in her attitude? You might also study the comic scene nearer the beginning, when Maggie is distracted by a radio call-in show at the body shop, and so gets hit by a truck as she is pulling out. What makes the scene funny? How does the author control the pace?

The memorial service is another good scene sequence to

study. Here you have several big scenes and some very funny moments. Again, the section has the arc of a story. Start by identifying the beginning, middle, and end of the *sequence;* then choose one of the scenes within the middle and study its structure.

Later, Maggie schemes to get Fiona to the house at the same time as Jesse, even though she has to know that Jesse has no interest in Fiona. The dinner scene is brilliant. Use what you have learned to figure out how and why it works so well.

Throughout the novel, pay attention to the way dialogue is handled—how different each character sounds, one from the other, and what attributions the author uses.

BODILY HARM *by Margaret Atwood*

A young journalist, Rennie, has gone to the Caribbean, trying to pull herself together emotionally, but her idyll is disrupted by tourists and terrorists. It's a scary, sometimes brutal, sometimes comic novel composed almost entirely of compact, highly charged scenes, many of them exploring power's place in sexual politics. What Rennie needs is compassion, if not love, and what she gets is menace, dread, and a scouring of her selfhood. It's instructive to see the meaning of sex in Atwood's suspenseful novel.

BIRDS OF AMERICA *by Lorrie Moore*

Gail Caldwell, book critic for the *Boston Globe,* called this collection of twelve stories "tough, lean, funny, and metaphysical." I would add various. Each story is worth studying, and you'll find every one crafted differently from the others.

Moore has said that awkwardness is where the tension is, and tension is where the story is. Watch for the awkwardness of these characters, their doomed fragility, their haplessness, their flailing about, and how much you love them. Take a scene, any scene, and spell out what these characters actually *do,* because

Moore is so very good at making actions peculiar and yet eerily familiar. Take a page and go sentence by sentence; every one is interesting. She wastes no words on getting there; she's always there.

"Community Life," about the Romanian Olena, is the "easiest" structure to grasp, a fairly straightforward chronology with some reflection about the past. Look at "Real Estate," to see how the threads of different trajectories come together. Moore sets up two lines of story to cross, escalating tension exponentially. A girlfriend makes Noel feel worthless because he doesn't know any songs, so he starts breaking into houses and forcing people to teach him verses. Meanwhile, an unrelated character, Ruth, buys a house full of trouble ranging from bats to break-in teenagers. Lo and behold, Noel's and Ruth's paths cross and the tension explodes into catastrophe.

Look for these elements in her stories:

- Places where she shows characters "being who they are," in "static scenes," rather than in scenes with event. She does this, as many writers do, in short passages among the storyline beats.

- The way she carries the memories of old events through a story line, so that they pop up again and again.

- The many different ways she opens passages and scenes.

- The way that the narrator's observations of life are part of a story, as well as what is happening.

- The way the fabric of the story is woven around character decisions. See especially "Willing." Make a list of the choices that Charlotte makes; study the situations that give rise to her decisions.

- How these stories are rich with the sense of scenes—always the feeling that you've seen odd things, you've watched people living their crazy, inevitable lives, past and present. Details are always perfect, surprising, jarring. In every story, it's not just what is going on, it's what has been going on for a while colliding with something else.

- Pick your favorite story and really, really get to know how it is put together. Find the focal points, those turns in the story that shift possibilities irrevocably. See if there is a pattern of accidents, choices, or discoveries. Use all the concepts from this book to talk about it. Find at least one thing you can take away from Lorrie Moore, not to be like her, but to be more like you.

NOTES

INTRODUCTION: THE READING WRITER

xii **She connects this habit to her ideas:** Alice Munro talks about this in "How I Write Stories," in Ann Charters, *The Story and Its Writer: An Introduction to Short Fiction,* 6th ed. (Bedford/St. Martin's, 2003). This anthology has a section of commentaries on craft. Copies are usually available in college bookstores.

xii **Many esteemed writers have paid homage:** See, for example, *Tributes: American Writers on American Writers: Conjunctions 29* (Bard College, 1997). See also Joyce Carol Oates's excellent essay "Reading As a Writer" in *On Writing Short Stories,* ed. Tom Bailey (Oxford University Press, 1999). Oates discusses the writer-mentor relationships I mention and many others.

xiv **Except for E. M. Forster:** See, for example, the recent book *Master Class in Fiction Writing: Techniques from Austen, Hemingway, and Other Greats* by Adam Sexton (McGraw-Hill, 2005).

xvii **That faculty comprises a love of storytelling:** Indeed, I recommend that you engage in collecting and telling stories frequently. Watch the newspaper, listen to the talk of your acquaintances, and so on; keep a notebook. If you have a group of writer friends, get together once a month to tell stories. Simply capture the heart of the tale: what happened to whom or who did what, with what consequences; what the story means to you. You want to build a repertoire of ideas and illustrations of human nature; you want to practice the telling of narratives. Write a page or two for each story, and soon you will have a catalog of stories. The monthly magazine *The Sun* has a section of reader contributions around a different theme each month that perfectly illustrates the power of short, true narratives and how they suggest ideas for fiction. I've also found *Writing for Your Life* by Deena Metzger (HarperSan-Francisco, 1992) to be quite useful to my students as a way to survey stories from one's own life.

1 THE BASICS

13   ***The screenwriter Christopher Keane:*** Keane's excellent book is called *How to Write a Selling Screenplay* (Broadway Books, 1998).

13   ***there is an idea or force connecting:*** One of the best discussions of this I know is Jane Smiley's in her engaging *Thirteen Ways of Reading the Novel* (Knopf, 2005). She says that a novel is a "theory of being," and that the writer argues it through assertion, sensation, and emotion.

2 EVENT AND MEANING

22   ***The protagonist acts and is affected:*** The protagonist is the character we care most about: the center of gravity of the story. *The protagonist does not have to be the POV character.* The POV character is the consciousness of the story. A famous example is the first-person-narrator novel *The Great Gatsby,* by F. Scott Fitzgerald (Scribner, 2004). The narrator is Nick Carraway but the protagonist is Gatsby. I like the discussion of point of view in *The Modern Library Writer's Workshop: A Guide to the Craft of Fiction* by Stephen Koch (Modern Library, 2003). The book is a treasure trove of wisdom and advice by the former chair of Columbia University's creative writing program. There is an especially good discussion of the stages of work in writing a novel.

23   ***Every scene in "Marie":*** Edward P. Jones, *Lost in the City* (Amistad, 2004). Also in *The Scribner Anthology of Contemporary*

Short Fiction, ed. Lex Williford and Michael Martone (Touchstone, 1999). (Hereafter, Scribner Stories.) Note that this scene has a classic story structure: a beginning (Marie encounters a mugger who tries to rob her), middle (accidentally cut by her knife, the mugger is shocked and infuriated but she stands up to him), and end (he goes away and she responds to the emotional aftereffects of the incident).

25   **big things going on in Ron Hansen's:** From Ron Hansen, *Nebraska: Stories* (Grove/Atlantic, 1989). Also in the anthology *The Vintage Book of Contemporary Short Stories,* ed. Tobias Wolff (Vintage, 1994). (Hereafter, Vintage Stories.)

26   **"Tall Tales from the Mekong Delta":** From Kate Braverman, *Squandering the Blue*. In Vintage Stories.

27   **a story of mine:** From "An Easy Pass," published in the online journal *Dragonfire*.

29   **In Stuart Dybek's "Pet Milk":** From *The Coast of Chicago* by Stuart Dybek (FSG, 1990). Also in Scribner Stories. Note that this passage is a reflection or response to the minor moment— the apprehension of the boy on the platform—that follows the action of the scene and assigns it meaning. This is a classic example of a reflective response at the end of a story.

35   **In Frank Conroy's classic collection of stories:** Frank Conroy, *Midair* (Penguin, 1993). I highly recommend this collection of stories.

39   **enough action and meaning to suggest:** Rust Hills, in his practical guide, *Writing in General and the Short Story in Particular* (Houghton Mifflin, 2000), says "We tend to encounter characters in fiction at a time of stress in their lives." He points out that when a protagonist is introduced into the action of a story, we should know right away that he is going to be significantly affected by the story's action. This is the second meaning of having something "happen" in a story: There is an effect on the main character.

39   ***A woman comes home from a trip:*** Wonderful story in which
      this happens: Lorrie Moore's "Real Estate," in *Birds of America*
      (Picador, 1999).

39   ***An adult child arrives home to the bedside:*** A story on this very
      theme is Ethan Canin's "The Year of Getting to Know Us" in
      Emperor of the Air (Mariner Books, 1999). Also in Scribner Sto-
      ries. The story has an elegant construction that balances three
      separate lines of chronology. Another, very different story on
      this theme, beautiful and complex, is John L'Heureux's "De-
      partures," discussed on pp. 77–78, which you can find in Vin-
      tage Stories. A priest comes home to await his mother's death
      and to deal with the memory of his bad behavior with her
      years earlier. Also in Vintage Stories you can find Susan Power's
      "Moonwalk," in which Margaret Many Wounds is dying, and
      her prodigal daughter comes back to the reservation. The story
      is composed almost entirely of scenes and is a good introduc-
      tion to Power's special vision.

3 BEATS

45   ***from "Daughter of the Moon" by Janet Peery:*** In *Alligator
      Dance* (SMU Press, 1993).

4 THE FOCAL POINT

55   ***See Charles Baxter's discussion:*** "Against Epiphanies," in Charles
      Baxter, *Burning Down the House: Essays on Fiction* (Graywolf, 1998).

5 PULSE

59   ***An immigrant bride:*** Two wonderful books with this theme:
      Bharati Mukherjee's novel *Jasmine* (Grove, 1999) and Elena
      Lappin's book of stories, *Foreign Brides* (Picador, 2000).

62   ***Raymond Carver's famous story:*** "Cathedral," from *Cathedral*
      (Vintage, 1989). Included in Vintage Stories.

63   ***Andre Dubus's story:*** "The Fat Girl," from *Adultery and Other
      Choices* (Godine, 1999). Included in Vintage Stories.

66   ***Anthony Doerr's exquisite story:*** Anthony Doerr, "The
      Hunter's Wife," from *The Shell Collector* (Scribner, 2002).

6 TENSION

74   ***his short story "Helping":*** Robert Stone's story was originally
      published in *The New Yorker*. It is reprinted in Vintage Stories.

76   ***Paul Bowles's unforgettable story:*** "A Distant Episode" has been
      widely anthologized and is included in *The Stories of Paul Bowles*
      (HarperPerennial, 2003). Robert Stone wrote the introduction.

76   ***the ferocious Mary Gaitskill:*** Start with *Bad Behavior: Vintage
      Contemporaries* (Vintage, 1989).

76   ***Joy Williams:*** See *Honored Guest: Stories* (Knopf, 2004).

76   ***Lynn Freed's fiction:*** See *House of Women: A Novel* (Back Bay
      Books, 2003). She has also written an excellent book of essays
      about the writing life, *Reading, Writing, and Leaving Home: A
      Life on the Page* (Harcourt, 2005).

77   ***John L'Heureux's story:*** Included in Vintage Stories.

79   ***<u>Emma didn't even bother</u>:*** From the novel *Plain Seeing* by San-
      dra Scofield (HarperCollins, 1997).

81   ***Lara Vapnyar's delightful story:*** From *There Are Jews in My
      House* (Pantheon, 2003).

86   ***Dan Chaon nicely illustrates:*** From *Among the Missing* (Bal-
      lantine, 2001).

7 NEGOTIATION

92   ***the complications and subtleties of story:*** Carol Bly, *The Pas-
      sionate, Accurate Story: Making Your Heart's Truth into Literature*
      (Milkweed, 1998).

92   ***"... the revelation of something not comprehended ...":*** Oak-
      ley Hall, *The Art & Craft of Novel Writing* (Story Press, 1994).

96   ***her wonderful story "Saint Chola":*** K. Kvashay-Boyle, "Saint
      Chola," from *The Best American Nonrequired Reading 2003,* ed.

Zadie Smith and Dave Eggers (series ed.) (Houghton Mifflin, 2003). An annual series of various genres from the glossies, chosen by Bay Area teenagers.

98   ***Annette Sanford's story "Housekeeping":*** from *Crossing Shattuck Bridge* (SMU Press, 1999).

102   ***This one is called "Nice Girl":*** From Victoria Lancelotta, *Here in the World: 13 Stories* (Counterpoint Press, 2000).

8 IMAGES

108   ***a story, "Festival":*** From Victoria Lancelotta, *Here in the World: 13 Stories.*

111   ***"Ax of the Apostles":*** From Erin McGraw, *The Good Life: Stories.*

9 SCENE ACTIVITY AND CHARACTER RESPONSE

126   ***events can be "external signs . . .":*** Tolstoy says that these are the ways that one person hands to another, *through art,* the feelings he has lived through. You can read his essay, "What Is Art," in *The Writer's Craft,* ed. John Hersey (Knopf, 1981). Debra Sparks discusses his ideas and those of others about the use of sentiment in writing in her useful, nicely readable book *Curious Attractions: Essays on Fiction Writing* (University of Michigan Press, 2005).

129   ***story "A Man of the Country":*** From Aaron Hamburger, *The View from Stalin's Head* (Random House, 2004).

11 BIG SCENES

171   ***Naipaul's* Half a Life:** Excerpted in V. S. Naipaul, *Vintage Naipaul* (Vintage, 2004).

171   ***"Lieutenant Mamiya's Long Story":*** From *Vintage Murakami* (Vintage, 2004). Best, really, that you read all of Part I and Part II and find the scene for yourself.

171 ***Baxter's story "Reincarnation":*** From Charles Baxter, *Believers: A Novella and Stories* (Vintage, 1998).

14 SCENARIOS

189 ***In Wichita Falls:*** From Sandra Scofield, *Plain Seeing* (Harper-Collins 1997).

190 ***book on writing:*** Elizabeth George, *Write Away: One Novelist's Approach to Fiction and the Writing Life* (Harper Paperbacks, 2005).

194 ***"enter the dream":*** John Gardner, *The Art of Fiction: Notes on Craft for Young Writers* (Vintage, 1991). Gardner says, "What counts in conventional fiction must be the vividness and continuity of the fiction dream the words set off in the reader's mind."

SAMPLE SCENES

195 **More Than Allies:** Sandra Scofield (Permanent Press, 1993).

204 **Opal on Dry Ground:** Sandra Scofield (Villard, 1997).

211 ***"Shout":*** From *Woodcuts of Women* by Dagoberto Gilb (Grove/Atlantic, 2001).

218 ***"Cartography of a Heart":*** From *The Necessary Grace to Fall* by Gina Ochsner (University of Georgia Press, 2002).

PERMISSIONS

FOR THE BEST IN PAPERBACKS, LOOK FOR THE 🐧

In every corner of the world, on every subject under the sun, Penguin represents quality and variety—the very best in publishing today.

For complete information about books available from Penguin—including Penguin Classics and Puffins—and how to order them, write to us at the appropriate address below. Please note that for copyright reasons the selection of books varies from country to country.

In the United States: Please write to *Penguin Group (USA), P.O. Box 12289 Dept. B, Newark, New Jersey 07101-5289* or call 1-800-788-6262.

In the United Kingdom: Please write to *Dept. EP, Penguin Books Ltd, Bath Road, Harmondsworth, West Drayton, Middlesex UB7 0DA.*

In Canada: Please write to *Penguin Books Canada Ltd, 90 Eglinton Avenue East, Suite 700, Toronto, Ontario M4P 2Y3.*

In Australia: Please write to *Penguin Books Australia Ltd, P.O. Box 257, Ringwood, Victoria 3134.*

In New Zealand: Please write to *Penguin Books (NZ) Ltd, Private Bag 102902, North Shore Mail Centre, Auckland 10.*

In India: Please write to *Penguin Books India Pvt Ltd, 11 Panchsheel Shopping Centre, Panchsheel Park, New Delhi 110 017.*

In the Netherlands: Please write to *Penguin Books Netherlands bv, Postbus 3507, NL-1001 AH Amsterdam.*

In Germany: Please write to *Penguin Books Deutschland GmbH, Metzlerstrasse 26, 60594 Frankfurt am Main.*

In Spain: Please write to *Penguin Books S. A., Bravo Murillo 19, 1° B, 28015 Madrid.*

In Italy: Please write to *Penguin Italia s.r.l., Via Benedetto Croce 2, 20094 Corsico, Milano.*

In France: Please write to *Penguin France, Le Carré Wilson, 62 rue Benjamin Baillaud, 31500 Toulouse.*

In Japan: Please write to *Penguin Books Japan Ltd, Kaneko Building, 2-3-25 Koraku, Bunkyo-Ku, Tokyo 112.*

In South Africa: Please write to *Penguin Books South Africa (Pty) Ltd, Private Bag X14, Parkview, 2122 Johannesburg.*